W9-CSG-902

CHRISTMAS IN THE WEST

CHRISTMAS IN THE WEST

Hugh A Dempsey

Western Producer Prairie Books
Saskatoon, Saskatchewan

Edited by Candace Savage

Cover and book design by John Luckhurst/GDL

Printed and bound in Canada by Modern Press ⟨⟩ 1
Saskatoon, Saskatchewan

The cover illustration, entitled "Christmas in the Wilds with the Hudson's Bay Company Traders," is an 1877 engraving by Arthur Lumley.

Western Producer Prairie Book publications are produced and manufactured in the middle of western Canada by a unique publishing venture owned by a group of prairie farmers who are members of Saskatchewan Wheat Pool. From the first book published in 1954, a reprint of a serial originally carried in the weekly newspaper, *The Western Producer,* to the book before you now, the tradition of providing enjoyable and informative reading for all Canadians is continued.

Canadian Cataloguing in Publication Data
Main entry under title:
Christmas in the West

    Includes index.
    ISBN 0-88833-095-2

    1. Christmas — Canada, Western — History.
2. Canada, Western — Social life and customs.
I. Dempsey, Hugh A., 1929-
GT4987.15.C57   394.2'68282'09712
                C82-091248-4

To Mom
who gave me so many
wonderful Christmases

Just Before Christmas

Contents

Preface

hristmas is the time of year when a person thinks of family gatherings, decorated trees, turkey dinners, the Christ Child, gaily wrapped gifts, and the strains of "Silent Night." It is a season for happiness or loneliness, a time for memories, or for the events from which memories arise. It is the season for nostalgia, as we reflect upon the "good old days" when life was simpler and people celebrated the holy day without all the commercialism of today.

In this book, we look back upon those earlier Christmases. Some stories confirm our notion of the simple life of years gone by, yet commercialism has been with us since the beginning, as evidenced by the fact that our first advertisement from a western Canadian newspaper (promoting children's books for Christmas) dates from 1861. The old adage "The more things change, the more they remain the same" is true of Christmas. If anything, western Canadians should take heart at how much has remained constant. In spite of today's complex computer age, the philosophies of family and prayer have not entirely disappeared. Nor has the feeling that people want to be with their loved ones at Christmas, and are lonely and dejected if they cannot do so.

Christmas has touched the hearts of most people at one time or another, including many western Canadian authors. People like Nellie L. McClung, John McDougall, and James G. MacGregor join scores of other pioneers in this book who have been inspired to record some personal anecdote about the Yuletide season.

If one reads through old newspapers, he or she will be impressed by how much western Canadian history is revealed through recollections of the holiday season. The fur trader's life, the Red River Rebellion, Indian missions all take on an added dimension when Christmas comes into the picture. In fact, that is how this book came into existence. Historians spend many hours looking through old books and newspapers, searching for clues for their current studies. During this process, one inevitably encounters some vignette of history which may not be pertinent to the subject at hand but which is filed away for future reference. Over a period of years, I noticed that my file entitled "Christmas" was growing fatter and fatter. Finally, during a festive season, when feeling in the proper mood, I pulled it out and was both inspired by and pleased with what I read. Taken as a whole, the accounts reflected the spirit of Christmas as seen by the pioneers of western Canada. The next step was to share these stories with others.

The sources are diverse. Of course, they include artist Paul Kane's description of Christmas in 1847, for this is probably the most often-repeated story about a festive dinner. In fact, a group of Edmontonians reenacts the feast and the incident every year, right down to the entrées of beaver tail and moose nose. But there are many other tales which have never reappeared in print since they were published in some obscure newspaper or magazine a century ago. Still others are from manuscript sources.

In order to keep the stories pertinent to the theme, some editing and abridging has been necessary, but this has been kept to a minimum and changes made only to maintain clarity and accuracy. In each instance, the style and spirit of the original has been faithfully maintained.

I wish to thank a number of persons and institutions for the help given to me. First is my own institution, the Glenbow Museum, Calgary, both for its support and for access to the wonderful sources in its Library, Archives, and Art Department collections. Also, to the Provincial Archives of Manitoba, Saskatchewan Archives Board, Provincial Archives of Alberta, and Public Archives of Canada for sharing their treasures with me; to the various publishers and authors who have permitted their works to be reproduced; and to my wife, Pauline, for typing the manuscript.

And to you, the reader, a Merry Christmas!

Part I
The Fur Trade
Frontier

Christianity — and, with it, Christmas — came to the West with the first fur traders, but the church did not become institutionalized until the arrival of the missionaries in the first half of the nineteenth century. The Red River Settlement, sponsored by Lord Selkirk in 1811, gave the area its first agricultural community and laid the way for Winnipeg to become the business center of the West. After the transfer of Rupert's Land to the Dominion of Canada in 1869, the new government sent the North-West Mounted Police to bring law and order, negotiated treaties with the Indians, and arranged for the construction of the Canadian Pacific Railway to open the prairies for settlement. In the pre-railway era, the fur-trade frontier celebrated Christmas in its own traditional ways.

The Trade Shop

Christmas at York Factory, 1843

Robert M. Ballantyne served for six years as an apprentice clerk with the Hudson's Bay Company, mostly at York Factory on the shores of Hudson Bay. From his experiences he wrote the book Hudson's Bay; or Everyday Life in the Wilds of North America, first published in 1848, from which this extract is taken. Ballantyne returned to Scotland where he became a prolific author of children's books, producing an average of two novels a year for the next four decades. In his account of a fur-trade Christmas, Ballantyne identifies Post Master Robert Wilson by his correct name but uses pseudonyms for his fellow apprentice Thomas Charles (Crusty) and Chief Trader James Hargraves (Mr. Grave).

As the Christmas holidays approached, we prepared for the amusements of that joyous season. On the morning before Christmas, a gentleman, who had spent the first part of the winter all alone at his outpost, arrived to pass the holidays at York Factory. We were greatly delighted to have a new face to look at, having seen no one but ourselves since the ship left for England, nearly four months before.

Our visitor had travelled in a dog cariole. This machine is very narrow, just broad enough to admit one person. It is a wooden frame covered with deer-skin parchment, painted gaudily, and is generally drawn by four Esquimaux dogs.

Christmas morning dawned, and I opened my eyes to behold the sun flashing brightly on the window in its endeavours to make a forcible entry into my room through the thick hoar-frost which covered the panes. Presently I became aware of a gentle breathing near me and, turning my eyes slowly round, I beheld my companion Crusty standing on tiptoe, with a tremendous grin on his countenance, and a huge pillow in his hands, which was in the very act of descending upon my devoted head. To collapse into the smallest possible compass, and present the most invulnerable part of my body to the blow, was the work of an instant, when down came the pillow, bang!

"Hooroo! hurroo! hurroo! a merry Christmas to you, you rascal!" shouted Crusty.

Medicine Hat News,
December 20, 1894.

Bang! bang! went the pillow.

"Turn out of that, you lazy lump of plethoric somnolescence," whack! — and, twirling the ill-used pillow round his head, my facetious friend rushed from the room, to bestow upon the other occupants of the hall a similar salutation. Upon recovering from the effects of my pommelling, I sprang from bed and donned my clothes with all speed, and then went to pay my friend Mr. Wilson the compliments of the season. In passing through the hall for this purpose, I discovered Crusty struggling in the arms of the skipper, who, having wrested the pillow from him, was now endeavouring to throttle him partially. I gently shut and fastened the door of their room, purposing to detain them there till very nearly too late for

breakfast, and then sat down with Mr. Wilson to discuss our intended proceedings during the day. These were — firstly, that we should go and pay a ceremonious visit to the men; secondly, that we should breakfast; thirdly, that we should go out to shoot partridges; fourthly, that we should give a ball in Bachelors' Hall in the evening, to which were to be invited all the men at the fort, and all the Indians, men, women, and children, inhabiting the country for thirty

A nineteenth century engraving entitled "Christmas in Manitoba," shows a family arriving at a trading post with a dog team and cariole.

3

miles round. As the latter, however, did not amount to above twenty, we did not fear that more would come than our hall was calculated to accommodate.

Our Christmas dinner was a good one, in a substantial point of view; and a very pleasant one, in a social point of view. We ate it in the winter mess-room; and really (for Hudson Bay) this was quite a snug and highly decorated apartment. True, there was no carpet on the floor and the chairs were home-made; but then the table was mahogany, and the walls were hung round with several large engravings in bird's-eye maple frames. The stove, too, was brightly polished with black lead, and the painting of the room had been executed with a view to striking dumb those innocent individuals who had spent the greater part of their lives at outposts, and were, consequently, accustomed to domiciles and furniture of the simplest and most unornamental description.

On the present grand occasion the mess-room was illuminated by an argand lamp, and the table covered with a snow-white cloth, whereon reposed a platter containing a beautiful fat, plump wild goose, which had a sort of come-eat-me-up-quick-else-I'll-melt expression about it that was painfully delicious. Opposite to this smoked a huge roast of beef, to procure which one of our most useless draught oxen had been sacrificed. This, with a dozen of white patridges and a large piece of salt pork, composed our dinner. But the greatest rarities on the board were two large decanters of port wine and two smaller ones of Madeira. These were flanked by tumblers and glasses; and truly, upon the whole, our dinner made a goodly show.

"Come away, gentlemen," said Mr. Grave, as we entered the room and approached the stove where he stood, smiling with that benign expression of countenance peculiar to stout, good-natured gentlemen at this season, and at this particular hour. "Your walk must have sharpened your appetites; sit down, sit down. This way, doctor — sit near me; find a place, Mr. Ballantyne, beside your friend Crusty there; take the foot, Mr. Wilson;" and amid a shower of such phrases we seated ourselves and began.

At the top of the table sat Mr. Grave, indistinctly visible through the steam that rose from the wild goose before him. On his right and left sat the doctor and the accountant; and down from them sat the skipper, four clerks, and Mr. Wilson, whose honest face beamed with philanthropic smiles at the foot of the table. Loud were the mirth and fun that reigned on this eventful day within the walls of the highly decorated room at York Factory. Bland was the expression of Mr. Grave's face when he asked each of the young clerks to drink wine with him in succession; and great was the confidence which thereby inspired the said clerks, prompting them to the perpetration of several rash and unparalleled pieces of presumption — such as drinking wine with each other (an act of free-will on their part almost unprecedented), and indulging in sundry sly pieces of covert humour, such as handing the vinegar to each other when the salt was requested, and becoming profusely apologetic upon discovering their mistake. But the wildest storm is often succeeded by the

4

greatest calm, and the most hilarious mirth by the most solemn gravity. In the midst of our fun Mr. Grave proposed a toast. Each filled a bumper and silence reigned around while he raised his glass and said, "Let us drink to absent friends." We each whispered, "Absent friends," and set our glasses down in silence, while our minds flew back to the scenes of former days, and we mingled again in spirit with our dear, dear friends at home. How different the mirth of the loved ones there, circling round the winter hearth, from that of the men seated round the Christmas table in the Nor'-West wilderness! I question very much if this toast was ever drunk with a more thorough appreciation of its melancholy import than upon the present memorable occasion. Our sad feelings, however, were speedily put to flight, and our gravity routed, when the skipper, with characteristic modesty, proposed, "The ladies;" which toast we drank with a hearty good-will, although, indeed, the former included them, inasmuch as they also were absent friends — the only one within two hundred and fifty miles of us being Mr. Grave's wife.

What a magical effect ladies have upon the male sex, to be sure! Although hundreds of miles distant from an unmarried specimen of the species, upon the mere mention of their name there was instantly a perceptible alteration for the better in the looks of the whole party. Mr. Wilson unconsciously arranged his hair a little more becomingly, as if his lady-love were actually looking at him; and the skipper afterwards confessed that his heart had bounded suddenly out of his breast, across the snowy billows of the Atlantic, and come smash down on the wharf at Plymouth Dock, where he had seen the last wave of Nancy's checked cotton neckerchief as he left the shores of Old England.

Just as we had reached the above climax, the sound of a fiddle struck upon our ears and reminded us that our guests who had been invited to the ball were ready; so emptying our glasses, we left the dining-room and adjourned to the hall.

Here a scene of the oddest description presented itself. The room was lit up by means of a number of tallow candles stuck in tin sconces round the walls. On benches and chairs sat the Orkneymen and Canadian half-breeds of the establishment in their Sunday jackets and capotes; while here and there the dark visage of an Indian peered out from among their white ones. But round the stove — which had been removed to one side to leave space for the dancers — the strangest group was collected. Squatting down on the floor in every ungraceful attitude imaginable sat about a dozen Indian women dressed in printed calico gowns, the chief peculiarity of which was the immense size of the balloon-shaped sleeves and the extreme scantiness, both in length and width, of the skirts. Coloured handkerchiefs covered their heads and ornamented moccasins decorated their feet; besides which, each one wore a blanket in the form of a shawl, which they put off before standing up to dance.

They were chatting and talking to each other with great volubility, occasionally casting a glance behind them where at least half-a-dozen infants stood bolt upright in their tight-laced cradles. On a chair, in a corner near the stove, sat a young good-looking

Indian with a fiddle of his own making beside him. This was our Paganini; and beside him sat an Indian boy with a kettle-drum on which he tapped occasionally, as if anxious that the ball should begin.

All this flashed upon our eyes; but we had not much time for contemplating it as, the moment we entered, the women simultaneously rose and coming modestly forward to Mr. Wilson, who was the senior of the party, saluted him, one after another! I had been told that this was a custom of the *ladies* on Christmas day, and was consequently not quite unprepared to go through the ordeal. But when I looked at the superhuman ugliness of some of the old ones — when I gazed at the immense, and in some cases toothless, chasms that were pressed to my senior's lips, and that gradually, like a hideous nightmare, approached towards me, my courage forsook me, and I entertained for a moment the idea of bolting.

The doctor seemed to labour under the same disinclination with myself; for when they advanced to him, he refused to bend his head and, being upwards of six feet high, they of course were obliged to pass him. They looked, however, so much disappointed at this and withal so very modest, that I really felt for them and prepared to submit to my fate with the best grace possible. A horrible old hag advanced towards me, the perfect embodiment of a nightmare, with a fearful grin on her countenance. I shut my eyes. Suddenly a bright idea flashed across my mind; I stooped down, with apparent good-will, to salute her; but just as our lips were about to meet, I slightly jerked up my head, and she kissed my *chin*. Oh, happy thought! They were all quite satisfied, and attributed the accident, no doubt, to their own clumsiness — or to mine!

This ceremony over, we each chose partners, the fiddle struck up, and the ball began. Scotch reels were the only dances known by the majority of the guests, so we confined ourselves entirely to them.

The Indian women afforded us a good deal of amusement during the evening. Of all ungraceful beings they are the most ungraceful; and of all accomplishments, dancing is the one in which they shine least. There is no rapid motion of the feet, no lively expression of the countenance; but with a slow, regular, up-and-down motion, they stalk through the figure with extreme gravity. They seemed to enjoy it amazingly, however, and scarcely allowed the poor fiddler a moment's rest during the whole evening.

Between eleven and twelve o'clock our two tables were put together, and spread with several towels; thus forming a pretty respectable supper-table, which would have been perfect, had not the one part been three inches higher than the other. On it was placed a huge dish of cold venison, and a monstrous iron kettle of tea. This, with sugar, bread, and a lump of salt butter, completed the entertainment to which the Indians sat down. They enjoyed it very much — at least, so I judged from the rapid manner in which the viands disappeared, and the incessant chattering and giggling kept up at intervals. After all were satisfied, the guests departed in a state of great happiness; particularly the ladies, who tied up the remnants of their supper in their handkerchiefs, and carried them away.

Before concluding the description of our Christmas doings, I may as well mention a circumstance which resulted from the effects of the ball, as it shows in a curious manner the severity of the climate at York Factory. In consequence of the breathing of so many people in so small a room for such a length of time, the walls had become quite damp, and ere the guests departed moisture was trickling down in many places. During the night this moisture was frozen, and on rising the following morning I found, to my astonishment, that Bachelors' Hall was apparently converted into a palace of crystal. The walls and ceiling were thickly coated with beautiful minute crystalline flowers, not sticking flat upon them, but projecting outwards in various directions, thus giving the whole apartment a cheerful light appearance, quite indescribable. The moment our stove was heated, however, the crystals became fluid, and ere long evaporated leaving the walls exposed in all their original dinginess.

When Robert Ballentyne celebrated his first western Christmas at York Factory in 1843, he attended the ball which consisted exclusively of Scottish reels. An artist depicted this scene from the author's description.

Christmas at Fort Edmonton

One of the most famous descriptions of Christmas in western Canada was provided by Toronto artist Paul Kane, during a visit to Fort Edmonton in 1847. Kane was on a two-year-long journey to the Pacific coast and back, painting Indians and scenes along the way.

Moose Nose

Remove the nose from the moose's head and place in the coals of a hot fire until the hair is burned off, including the hair in the nostrils. The nose will be pure white after the hair comes off. Scrape all the hard stuff and boil the meat, adding spices, onions, or other vegetables to taste. Cooks quickly.

Some people let it hang for a few days before cooking to make it more tender, while others put it in a smokehouse for a day or two to give it a smoked flavour.

he fort at this time of the year presented a most pleasing picture of cheerful activity; every one was busy; the men, some in hunting and bringing in the meat when the weather permitted, some in sawing boards in the saw-pit, and building the boats, about thirty feet long and six feet beam, which go as far as York Factory, and are found more convenient for carrying goods on the Saskatchewan and Red River than canoes. They are mostly built at Edmonton, because there are more boats required to take the peltries to York Factory than is required to bring goods back; and more than one-half of the boats built here never return. This system requires them to keep constantly building.

The women find ample employment in making moccasins and clothes for the men, putting up pemmican in ninety-pound bags, and doing all the household drudgery, in which the men never assist them. The evenings are spent round their large fires in eternal gossiping and smoking. The sole musician of the establishment, a fiddler, is now in great requisition amongst the French part of the inmates, who give full vent to their national vivacity, whilst the more sedate Indian looks on with solemn enjoyment.

No liquor is allowed to the men or Indians; but the want of it did not in the least seem to impair their cheerfulness. True, the gentlemen of the fort had liquor brought out at their own expense; but the rules respecting its use were so strict and so well known, that none but those to whom it belonged either expected, or asked, to share it.

On Christmas day the flag was hoisted, and all appeared in their best and gaudiest style, to do honour to the holiday. Towards noon every chimney gave evidence of being in full blast, whilst savoury steams of cooking pervaded the atmosphere in all directions. About two o'clock we sat down to dinner. Our party consisted of Mr. Harriett, the chief, and three clerks, Mr. Thebo [Thibault], the Roman Catholic missionary from Manitou Lake, about thirty miles off, Mr. Rundell [Rundle], the Wesleyan missionary, who resided within the pickets, and myself, the wanderer, who, though returning from the shores of the Pacific, was still the latest importation from civilized life.

The dining-hall in which we assembled was the largest room in the fort, probably about fifty by twenty-five feet, well warmed by large fires, which are scarcely ever allowed to go out. The walls and ceilings are boarded, as plastering is not used, there being no limestone within reach; but these boards are painted in a style of the most startling barbaric gaudiness, and the ceiling filled with centre-pieces of fantastic gilt scrolls, making altogether a saloon

Fort Edmonton was the principal post on the upper Saskatchewan River, and was the center for Christmas activities. This is a view of the post during the Christmas season in 1871.

which no white man would enter for the first time without a start, and which the Indians always looked upon with awe and wonder.

The room was intended as a reception room for the wild chiefs who visited the fort; and the artist who designed the decorations was no doubt directed to "astonish the natives." If such were his instructions, he deserves the highest praise for having faithfully complied with them, although, were he to attempt a repetition of the same style in one of the rooms of the Vatican, it might subject him to some severe criticisms from the fastidious. No tablecloth shed its snowy whiteness over the board; no silver candelabra or gaudy china interfered with its simple magnificence. The bright tin plates and dishes reflected jolly faces, and burnished gold can give no truer zest to a feast.

Perhaps it might be interesting to some dyspeptic idler, who painfully strolls through a city park, to coax an appetite to a sufficient intensity to enable him to pick an ortolan, if I were to describe to him the fare set before us, to appease appetites nourished by constant outdoor exercise in an atmosphere ranging at 40° to 50° below zero. At the head, before Mr. Harriett, was a large dish of boiled buffalo hump; at the foot smoked a boiled buffalo calf.

Baked Beaver Tail

This recipe is taken from Rubaboo *by Dorine Thomas, published by Pemmican Publications of Winnipeg in 1981.*

Remove the beaver tail from the body of the animal. Dip it into boiling water to remove the outer skin, exposing the meat. To cook in a stone oven, place on a rack over a drip pan and bake ½ hour in a moderate oven. To cook over an open fire, skewer the tail on a green stick and cook slowly over coals.

This meat is very fat and rich and must be allowed to drip. Save the drippings to use over potatoes baked in their skins in an oven or campfire.

Facing page: In 1881 the *London Graphic* depicted various scenes of fur trade life in western Canada. The top panel shows Indians trading beaver, fish, and fowl, while the panel below depicts the raising of the Hudson's Bay Company flag on Christmas morning. The next three panels reveal the tribulation of a Scots trader making plum pudding, while the bottom scene shows fur trade employees at the Christmas ball.

Start not, gentle reader, the calf is very small, and is taken from the cow by the Caesarean operation long before it attains its full growth. This, boiled whole, is one of the most esteemed dishes amongst the epicures of the interior. My pleasing duty was to help a dish of mouffle, or dried moose nose; the gentleman on my left distributed, with graceful impartiality, the white fish, delicately browned in buffalo marrow. The worthy priest helped the buffalo tongue, whilst Mr. Rundell cut up the beavers' tails. Nor was the other gentleman left unemployed, as all his spare time was occupied in dissecting a roast wild goose. The centre of the table was graced with piles of potatoes, turnips, and bread conveniently placed, so that each could help himself without interrupting the labours of his companions. Such was our jolly Christmas dinner at Edmonton; and long will it remain in my memory, although no pies, or puddings, or blanc manges, shed their fragrance over the scene.

In the evening the hall was prepared for the dance to which Mr. Harriett had invited all the inmates of the fort, and was early filled by the gaily dressed guests. Indians, whose chief ornament consisted in the paint on their faces, voyageurs with bright sashes and neatly ornamented moccasins, half-breeds glittering in every ornament they could lay their hands on; whether civilized or savage, all were laughing, and jabbering in as many different languages as there were styles of dress. English, however, was little used, as none could speak it but those who sat at the dinner-table. The dancing was most picturesque, and almost all joined in it. Occasionally I, among the rest, led out a young Cree squaw, who sported enough beads round her neck to have made a pedlar's fortune, and having led her into the centre of the room, I danced round her with all the agility I was capable of exhibiting, to some highland-reel tune which the fiddler played with great vigour, whilst my partner with grave face kept jumping up and down, both feet off the ground at once, as only an Indian can dance. I believe, however, that we elicited a great deal of applause from Indian squaws and children, who sat squatting round the room on the floor. Another lady with whom I sported the light fantastic toe, whose poetic name was Cun-ne-wa-bum, or "One that looks at the Stars," was a half-breed Cree girl; and I was so much struck by her beauty, that I prevailed upon her to promise to sit for her likeness, which she afterwards did with great patience, holding her fan, which was made of the tip end of swan's wing with an ornamental handle of porcupine's quills, in a most coquettish manner.

After enjoying ourselves with such boisterous vigor for several hours, we all gladly retired to rest about twelve o'clock, the guests separating in great good humour, not only with themselves but with their entertainers.

BARTERING FOR THE CHRISTMAS DINNER

CHRISTMAS MORNING—HOISTING THE BRITISH FLAG

MAKING THE PUDDING

IT TURNED OUT RATHER RAW

AND INDIGESTIBLE

A HALF-BREED BALL

At Cumberland House

In 1853, Anglican missionary John Hunter recorded in his diary the events which took place at his Indian mission and schoolhouse. Cumberland House, on the Saskatchewan River west of the present The Pas, served a large population of Cree hunters and trappers.

As early as the 1820s, Indian converts to Christianity flocked to the missions for religious services.

ecember 21, 1853. During the week the Indians were coming in from all quarters, to be present with us on next Lord's-day; a great number have applied to me to be admitted to the Lord's table on Sunday next, being Christmas-day. After careful examination and instruction, I admitted 13 new communicants, and as all the Indians belonging to this Station are here, I look forward to a large attendance at the Lord's table.

At our usual evening prayer meetings during the week, the school room has been crowded, and my addresses have had reference to the Lord's Supper, warning and encouraging them to come to that holy ordinance, pointing out the importance of the rite, at the same time the necessity of due examination and preparation for the right reception thereof. I trust that they feel their own sinfulness and unworthiness, and will come in simple dependance upon the Saviour, looking to Him for pardon and acceptance, and earnestly praying to be strengthened and refreshed with Divine Grace from on High. May He condescend to bless His own ordinance to their souls, and build them up in their most holy faith, that year by year as this blessed season comes round, they may be found advancing on the divine life & moulded more & more into the image of their Saviour.

I have often had occasion to notice that they come long distances to attend the Lord's table; in this respect they would put to the blush many in my own country, for they think nothing of a fatiguing journey of more than 100 miles, walking in snow shoes, to be present on these highly prized occasions.

Dec. 24. After prayers this evening, we gave our usual Christmas present to the Indians, consisting of Tea, Sugar, Flour, Pimekan, Grease & White Fish, which Charles Thomas, Louis Constant & Chas. Cook divided out to the inmates of each house around the Station, about 30 in all. It occupied some time, but they all went home with their portions and were very grateful, as they are rather short of provisions.

Dec. 25. Lord's-day, Christmas-day. We commenced the day with our usual early prayer meeting at 7 O'Clock; the School room was crowded and I read in Cree, Matt: 1 chap: 18 ver: to the end, and made some practical remarks both on the birth and death of the Saviour, as they were about to commemorate His dying love at the Lord's table. About 90 children present at the Sunday school, and Miss Ross continues her valuable aid in instructing the children. We had full morning service in the Church and I never saw it better filled than on this occasion, nor the Indians neater or cleaner in their persons.

I preached from Matt: 21 and then administered the Lord's Supper to 100 Communicants, being the largest number who have communicated here; they filled round the rails 6 times, and both men & women were very neatly attired, & many of them received the elements with tears and trembling. On the hands of several stretched out to receive the sacred elements, I noticed the marks which they had received when in a state of Heathenism, but blessed be God they have been brought from darkness to light, and from the power of sin and Satan unto God. May they now be sealed by the Spirit as the servants of the living God & in the day of the Saviour be found among that great multitude which no man can number, clothed with white robes and palms in their hands.

After the evening service I baptized 2 Infants and then went over to administer the Lord's Supper to Alexander Chichester, who was prevented by sickness from being present at the Lord's table to day. At night I felt exhausted from the duties of the day, and the previous week; and perhaps ministering in a foreign language is more fatiguing than in one's own. But I bless God that He gives me health and strength to labour for Him & may He be pleased to pardon all my infirmities and accept my poor Service for His dear Son's sake! Amen.

On Christmas Day, 1853, Rev. John Hunter observed, "We had full morning service in the Church and I never saw it better filled than on this occasion." This engraving, showing services at Lac La Ronge, was made two years earlier.

Holidays at Edmonton

Born in Red River, Peter Erasmus studied for the ministry but gave it up in 1856 when he was attracted to the freedom and adventures of the prairies. Traveling west to Fort Pitt, he was engaged as interpreter by Methodist missionary Thomas Woolsey and accompanied him to Edmonton later in the year. Shortly after he arrived at the fort, the Christmas festivities began.

The factor assigned me a room with one of his workmen, William Borwick, a man of approximately my own age but who had been in service with the Company for several years, mostly at Edmonton. We were approaching the Christmas holidays and there was a growing excitement noticeable among the inmates of the fort. Bill and others spent their spare time making ready their best clothes. The preparations the week before Christmas took on a new tempo of activity. Every dog driver and team was rushing supplies of fish to the fort for the dog trains of the expected visitors. The factor engaged two of the Indians who had buffalo-running horses to go with me after fresh meat, with orders to bring nothing but the best. We returned in four days with our pack horses loaded with two fine cows.

It was the custom of Hudson's Bay officials to meet at Fort Edmonton during Christmas week, staying for New Year's Day. They discussed business concerned with the trade, and prepared their orders for the following year. The conference had developed into a week of social activities commemorating the Christmas period.

Fort Pitt, Slave Lake, Chipewyan, Fort Assiniboine, Jasper House, Rocky Mountain House, and Lac La Biche were all represented. The two days before Christmas was a bedlam of noise as each new dog team arrived. Every arrival was a signal for all the dogs of the fort and those of the Crees camped nearby to raise their voices in a deafening uproar of welcome or defiance as their tempers dictated.

The noise was terrific, yet none of the regular inmates paid any attention or made any effort to silence any dog within reach. The drivers of the dog teams and the factors were assigned quarters as quickly as they arrived; the arrangements for the guests was a wonderful example of organized planning.

On Christmas Eve, Father Lacombe drove in to conduct Midnight Mass. I was somewhat surprised that the priest and my employer were on such friendly and cordial terms. Woolsey went out to meet him and immediately invited him to his room, where they spent several hours of congenial conversation. Of course I was on hand to take care of his dogs, as the man drove his own team.

Knowing the Rev. Woolsey's strong views against dancing, I was reluctant to ask permission to attend the celebrations, but I was burning to go. It was getting late when the priest finally departed for his duties with Catholic members of his church, and I finally screwed up enough courage to face the man.

Mr. Woolsey was seated reading his Bible when I entered his small room. I was in such a hurry to have his verdict that I had prepared no opening speech, although he looked slightly surprised at my late visit. He asked me to be seated, then as if reading my mind or perhaps noticing my flustered condition, said, "So you are fond of dancing."

It was my turn to look surprised as I answered too quickly in a tone of voice much too loud for that small room, "Yes I am, and that is what I came to see you about. I want your permission to attend."

In 1854 an imaginative British artist produced this winter scene of the Canadian West. Notice that the man at right is putting his snowshoes on backwards.

Slightly smiling, he answered, "I surmised as much from this late visit. I have given the matter some thought, for you know my principles over dancing. However, you're a young man and need some recreation; your own conscience must be your guide. I have no objections, provided you conduct yourself as a gentleman. Drinking will be quite conspicuous in tomorrow's festivities and as my associate I will not permit your indulgence in this miserable business."

"I can promise you that I'll do no drinking whatever as I've cultivated no taste for liquor. You have my promise on both counts."

"Thank you, I accept both promises," and in an amused tone he added, "I hope you don't find them too heavy an obligation."

Wishing him the Season's Greetings, I bade him goodnight. Delighted with the interview I ran back to our room to tell Bill the happy news. I was greatly relieved. Had he refused, I would have been in a difficult position. Bill was still up awaiting my return and I asked him what would be the order of the day.

"Well, many will be quite jolly as it is the custom for each of the employees to receive a ration of rum the day before Christmas, but by a rule of the Company no-one is to touch it before the next day. There will also be a dance at night; most of the women will come from the two settlements, Lac Ste. Anne and St. Albert. Let me assure you that some of the best-looking women in the West, and for that matter anywhere else, will be at that dance tomorrow night."

Then I told him of the wonderful news of receiving Woolsey's permission to attend. I danced a few steps for his benefit. Of course I did not tell him about the promise to abstain from drinking. I wanted all the credit to myself about being a gentleman. That always comes natural to a sober man for I have noticed that some of the most polished gentlemen lose some of their colour under the influence of drink.

It was some time before I was able to get to sleep, then suddenly it was morning. I was aroused from a deep sleep by a tremendous bloodcurdling noise that actually seemed to vibrate the room. For a moment I was shocked motionless, then the notes of music sounded into my senses. I was out of bed and scrambled for my clothes. Bill was already half dressed.

John Graham, a Scottish employee, burst into the room, almost incoherent with excitement and fairly dancing in his joy. Finally he shouted at the top of his voice, "The Pibroch! The Pibroch!" Tears coursed down his cheeks as he motioned for Bill and me to come. We dressed in seconds that morning and followed him out as he turned and dashed for the door.

Striding back and forth on the walk that surrounded three sides of the factor's three-storied building was a man by the name of Colin Fraser playing a set of bagpipes. The long droning notes that precede the actual music were what awakened me so suddenly. He made a striking figure, dressed in all the gay regalia of tartan and kilt, his knees exposed to the elements. He seemed quite indifferent to the weather that was at least thirty degrees below zero. The deep notes of his instrument echoed back from the high hills of the ice-covered Saskatchewan River. It was beautiful even to my unfamiliar ear; never till then had I heard the bagpipes played.

I turned to watch to face of our old friend [Graham] and felt some of the deep loneliness that marked the features of this old man, whose life ambition had been to return to his native land; he now realized he was too late ever to attain it. He stood with his hand on Borwick's shoulder; unashamed tears flowed down his cheeks. That night Bill and I carried him to his room, too inebriated to manage his own way.

Shortly after breakfast a horn was sounded, a sign that the factor was ready to receive the salutations of the men at the fort.

I accompanied Borwick in this customary courtesy. After greeting each man in turn the chief clerk, who stood at the factor's elbow for this purpose, handed each man a drink of rum. I watched Bill out of the corner of my eyes as I took my turn to shake hands and offer the factor the happy returns of the day. When I refused my offer of a drink, I could see consternation and anger on Bill's face. We were scarcely out of the room when he gave me a sound going over for refusing the drink.

"Look here, Peter! You have been guilty of a grave discourtesy in refusing a drink. This has been the custom of the Company since the memory of the oldest man in the service."

"My dear sir, I'm not an employee of your grand Company; my first duty is to my employer. The matter of the minister's man refusing a drink of rum will, I hope, not create a revolution in the service. Perhaps you'd better interview Mr. Woolsey before the situation gets too serious."

He gave me a disgusted look but said no more. However, I noticed that he made a great fuss and ceremony when it came time to open his own ration in our room and never offered me a courtesy drink that he had so strongly advocated early that morning. Up to this time and for several years afterwards, I had no desire for strong drink nor had occasion to test its possibilities, but regret to say that at this late date, I'm afraid I could not claim that boast.

Christmas day was spent in visiting among those gathered at the fort. Woolsey held a service in English which everybody attended, regardless of affiliation. I was not called up to interpret but sat with his audience.

I had heard stories of unrestricted convivial times at these Christmas gatherings but there was no evidence of excess that day, other than our friend Graham who appeared to be under no obligation to share his portion with any other of the workmen. He gave Bill a drink but when I refused mine, he took an extra for himself, first holding the glass high in the air in my direction, smacking his lips in anticipation, then sipping with evident relish, nodding his head towards me with an air of admiring approval as if my refusal was a personal act of kindness to himself.

The dance that night I thought upheld Bill's claims; in fact he had slightly underrated it. Borwick, being an old-timer in the area, seemed to know every person there and soon made me acquainted

17

with a number of his friends. They were friendly and cordial and called me by my first name without the formal use of surname. When Bill introduced me as Peter, I drew him aside and pointed out his omission.

"Heck, every one around here knows you as Erasmus, the minister's man, so why waste time? It's the custom around here to use first names or nicknames. They would think you were trying to put on airs if I called you Mr. Erasmus. Only factors, ministers of the church, and priests have a handle to their names."

Colours in clothes were quite in evidence but nothing so startling as in later years. The Hudson's Bay stores at that time were more conservative in their choices of colours and they were the only source of supply. Therefore dress in those days gave more attention to utility than fashion. Neatness of apparel was of primary importance and the winsome maids of the prairie were quite as adept at adjusting the means at hand as their sisters a quarter of a century later.

A big lunch was served at midnight in the homes of the married couples, where the guests had previously left their contributions of

Dancing was an important part of holiday festivities at early trading posts. This is an 1859 view of a ball at Pembina.

18

food at the homes of their friends and acquaintances. Young bachelor residents of the post were pressed into service as chore boys, regardless of their wishes in the matter. I presumed that usage had established a precedent; at any rate I found that single men were mere appendages of the wives' organization for entertaining their guests; we were errand boys. Bill's apparent enjoyment of my hesitant and clumsy handling of the job was plain to see. Wherever there was a shortage of any particular food, we were sent to a neighbouring house for supplies and we were both too busy to share in the talk and pleasantry going on wherever we went.

I was getting quite rebellious and said so in a low tone to Bill, who just laughed and told me to have a little more patience. At last the guests were all served and started drifting back to the dance floor. Most of the crowd had taken their food standing up around the tables. Not us; we were seated at a table with our hostess and the husband who from some hidden secret place brought out a sadly depleted bottle. Bill's malicious grin and wink was a determining factor in stiffening my weakened resistance.

Three attractive young ladies kept us supplied with food and talk; I refused the drink but needed no second invitation to start on the food. Under these circumstances I regained my good humour and for revenge on Bill, entered into a gay conversation with our attentive and pretty waitresses. Bill's devotion to the bottle left him badly handicapped in that competition.

There was very little rest for the musicians between dances, and there were plenty of fiddlers among the French Metis people from Lac Ste. Anne. Having too good a time dancing I did not offer my services that night, but later on I happened to mention to Bill that I liked playing the fiddle, and thereafter on Borwick's insistence I had to do my share.

The settlement guests all left for their homes at broad daylight. After dancing all night they had to run behind dogs for another forty miles before they would have any rest or sleep. The men were tough athletes to stand a grind like that and I did not envy their trip under those conditions.

The more serious business of the post leaders was of course not neglected for any of the social events at the fort or at the settlements. The conference was brought to a final grand finish with New Year's Day sports. There were foot races, toboggan slides on the North Saskatchewan River hill, some competitions for the women, and the big dog-train race of three miles on the river. Every team from each post competed in this race. Each factor contributed a share to this prize; the winner took all, which was a choice of any clothes in stock to the amount of approximately twenty-five dollars.

The employed dog drivers for the Company at Edmonton asked the factor if they could allow me to drive one of their two dog teams. He consented, provided the other leaders agreed. They readily consented as they considered me poor competition against their own hardened and skillful drivers.

Bill heard about the arrangement and came to me with the

intention of talking me out of it. "Man, you haven't a chance in the world against these men from Jasper House and Athabasca; fifty miles a day is a regular run for them. They would be ashamed if they were caught riding. They are tough, strong young men. Heck, man! That's all they know, just running behind dogs all winter."

"Bill, I'm going to beat every last one of them; I'll tell you how I aim to do it. Every driver has been idle, eating and drinking to the limit of his capacity all week. Their dogs are the same, and will be in no fit condition for a short fast race like this will be. Our dogs are in work shape. The team I drive has made a trip to Lac Ste. Anne this week; they are not overfed and they are rested enough to be keen in tomorrow's run. Bet your shirt, Bill; if you lose, I'll give you one of mine. Besides, I don't drink and that's my biggest lead over all the others."

This latter remark was just a dig for Bill's private opinions on drinking, but I had considerable faith in my ability as a runner, for I had won foot races against some pretty strong competition. My trips for the post after game and fish had kept me in good condition. Pierre, the driver of the second team, had urged me to enter the race and had been the one to approach the factor.

"Peter, you by gar, are de best runner in dese parts. You win de race for sure. You never drink de whisky, while dem men dey drink, dey eat an' feed de dogs like peegs. Dey lazy like Hell, all de week. For sure you win dat race, maybe."

The starting point was marked by stakes frozen in the ice far enough apart to accommodate the seven teams at the line. One mile and a half downriver was another set of stakes, three in number around which we must drive before returning to the starting line. Failure to pass around the far stake would disqualify any driver. There were judges at this end and watchers at the other to make sure the drivers complied with the rules. No man was allowed to foul up another driver or cut in unless he had a clear lead to the trail that would be well marked on our trip downriver.

We were off! Bill was my helper at the post. I had given him instructions to hold the dogs back until at least half of the others had started. They would be ploughing snow on an untravelled track. Bill, disgusted at that foolish way of starting, nevertheless obeyed. There were four teams in the lead, all abreast for the first two hundred yards or so. The Jasper man had the same idea as I had; he was holding his dogs to the track already made by the other four toboggans. One man was left at the post as his dogs in their eagerness had become fouled up in their harness. I could see that the man from Jasper would be my strong competitor.

What none of the other drivers knew about was a stretch of overflow ice on the last half mile of the course downriver where I hoped to pass the others without plowing deep snow. Pierre, our Edmonton driver, was now in second place behind the Fort Pitt man. We were all closely bunched when we made the turn but I got ahead of the fourth team as his dogs cut short instead of rounding the marker posts, and he had to turn his dogs.

I was now in third place, the Jasper man directly behind me.

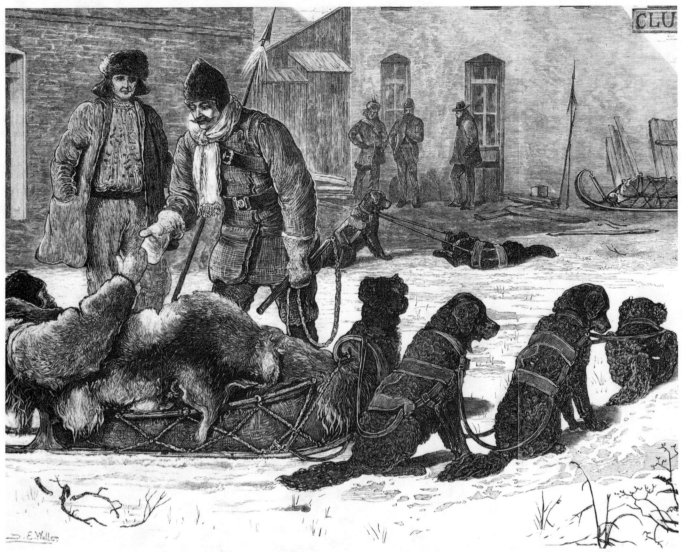

When I came opposite the overflow ice, I struck into the deep snow as if to pass the team ahead; he started to follow me but seeing the depth of snow turned back. The minute I reached the thin snow on the overflow ice, I cracked the whip over the dogs' backs and yelled. They almost threw me off the sleigh with their increased speed, as I had climbed on the sleigh to give it weight.

Now ahead of all the others, I allowed myself plenty of room before cutting back to the track. I had the race if I could stand the pace that I was being forced to travel to hold my lead. I had a brief breather while riding the overflow but jumped off when I came to the now wellmarked trail.

The Fort Pitt man was close up behind me and I knew I had to outdistance him before we reached the last quarter mile, because then he would also have a broken trail to follow. Now for the second time since starting I cracked my whip over the dogs, yelling for more speed, not hitting them but my voice and whip urging more speed.

I did not dare to look behind me at the others but was content with side glances only. For truth to tell, I had no breath to spare nor energy to worry about opponents as long as I could see no driver

During the Christmas season, fur traders traveled for many miles to congregate at the larger posts. This engraving, published in the *London Graphic* in 1876, shows a trader arriving at Fort Garry.

21

A Fur-Trading Post.

Going to Church.

The Mail Carrier.

Fishing through the Ice.

ahead. We were only a hundred yards or so from the starting posts when another side glance showed the Fort Pitt man gaining beside me, his lead dog almost opposite my toboggan front. Only the short distance would save the race for me as I had the limit of speed out of my dogs. I hit the finish line with only a two dog advantage over my opponent.

Bill was like a crazy man, shouting and yelling his triumph for my win, but I found out later his delight was for himself as he had won a new shirt and pants by betting on my team to win. He even forgot to congratulate me as all the others did as soon as I could get my breath to acknowledge my thanks. Pierre and the Jasper man had fought for third place but the Jasper man beat him in a closer finish than my win. In fact the judges had some doubt about it but Pierre acknowledged his defeat. He told me afterwards, by gar, he didn't care as long as our Edmonton team won a first.

At daylight the next morning the far-distant post managers had pulled out for another long year of isolated wilderness where their duties held little of entertainment and no social life whatever, until the following gathering a year hence at Edmonton. No wonder the Chief Factor had put so much effort and attention for their comfort and entertainment while they were in Edmonton.

Facing page: In 1883 an artist for *Harper's Weekly* depicted these "Winter scenes in the Northwest."

These resting teams were sketched in 1884.

Christmas in the Dog Days

John McDougall, the son of a Methodist missionary, came West to join his father in 1860 at the age of eighteen; later he became a missionary himself. He was an exhuberant, robust man who gloried in the challenges of the frontier and was impatient with those whom he perceived to be weak or unsuited to the life. The man Woolsey whom he criticizes in this account is the same person whom Peter Erasmus mentions favorably in his Christmas story. McDougall later became the author of numerous books on missionary life and his own adventures in the West. The "Smoking Lake" mentioned in this excerpt is today known as Smoky Lake, Alberta.

t is now near Christmas, 1862, and Mr. Woolsey planned to spend the holidays at Edmonton. We left [Smoking Lake mission] long before daylight the Monday morning before Christmas, which came on Thursday that year. We had about four inches of snow to make our road through. This was hardly enough for good sleighing, but where there was prairie or ice, our dogs had good footing and made good time.

Down the slope of country to Smoking Lake, and then along the full length of the lake we went; then straight across country, over logs and round the windings of the dim bridlepath for the Wah-suh-uh-de-now, or "Bay in the Hills" (which would bring us to the Saskatchewan River), to which place we came about daylight, having already made a good thirty-five miles of our journey. Mr. Woolsey had slept and snored most of the way. What cared he for precipitous banks, or tortuous trails, or the long hours of night!

After coming down the big hill into the valley at a break-neck pace, we came to the almost perpendicular bank of the stream, still seventy-five or eighty feet high, and here I roused Mr. Woolsey, and asked him to climb down, while Williston and I took the dogs off and let the cariole and sled down as easily as we could.

Once down, we got Mr. Woolsey in again, and away we went up the river at a good smart run, my leader taking the way; from point to point, and around the rapids and open water at the word. For another five miles we kept on, and stopped for breakfast before sunrise opposite Sucker Creek.

To jerk these dogs out of their collars is the first thing. This gives them a chance to roll and run about, and supple up after the long pull of the morning. Then we make a big fire and cut some brush to put down in front of it; then help Mr. Woolsey out of his cariole, next boil the kettle, and roast our dried meat and eat. Then after a short prayer, and while the "Amen" is still on our lips, we hitch up the dogs, tie the sleigh, help Mr. Woolsey into cariole, tuck and wrap him in, and "Marse!" Away jump my dogs once more, and their bells ring out in the clear morning frost, and are echoed up and down the valley as we ascend, for even over the ice the ascension is very perceptible.

On we went, steadily making those long stretches of river which are between Sucker Creek and Vermilion. As we proceed, we left the snow, and the ice became glare and very difficult to run on, especially when one had to constantly steady the cariole to keep it from upsetting in the drift ice, or from swinging into the open channel. I slipped once badly, and gave myself a wrench, the effects of which I felt at times for many a long year.

After stopping for lunch on an island, we pushed on, and, climbing the hill at the mouth of Sturgeon River, found the country bare of snow, and after going two or three miles in this way, I concluded to camp, and strike back for the river in the morning.

If we could have gone on, we would have reached Edmonton the next day before noon.

Mr. Woolsey was astonished at our progress. We had come fully eighty miles, although the latter part of the road was very difficult to travel, the glare but uneven river ice being very hard on both dogs and men.

We camped on a dry bluff. What a revelation this country is to me! This is now the 22nd of December, and the weather, while crisp and cold, beautifully fine — no snow — and we having to use exceedingly great caution in order not to set the prairie on fire.

The next morning we struck straight across country for the river, and kept the ice thence on to Edmonton, which, because of the windings of the stream, we did not reach until evening. We found the fort full, trappers, and traders having returned from their long summer's journeyings; but we also found provisions scant, and Mr. Christie, the gentleman in charge, anxious as to the future. The buffalo were far out; the fisheries were not very successful.

Here we met with clerks and post-masters from the inland and distant posts, and we and they but added to the responsibilities of the head officer, having so many more mouths to feed. Then there were all the dogs, and these were simply legion, as most of the winter transport and travel of those days was done with dogs, and their food supply was a serious question.

I have often wondered since then why it was in a country with so much natural hay, where oats grew often at the rate of one hundred bushels to the acre, and where horses were cheap, that this dog business lasted as long as it did; but I suppose everything has its day, and even the dog had his.

I fully believe that if there was one dog in the small compass of

Making Camp

Hang on to them

Up Hill work

Now then on with that harness.

This view of "Life in Manitoba" and the tribulations of living in the "dog days" was prepared for *Harper's Weekly* in 1877.

the fort at Edmonton, there were one hundred and fifty. When the bell rang for the men to go to work or come for their rations, the dogs would howl, and one would imagine bedlam let loose. Then the fights, which were taking place at all hours, day or night, became monotonous.

The sole topic of conversation would be dogs. The speed and strength and endurance of a dog-train occupied the thoughts of most men, either sleeping or waking.

Next to the dogs came the dog-runners. These were famous because of their ability to manage a train of dogs, and the wind and endurance and pluck they manifested in travel.

Races were common — five miles, twenty miles, sixty miles, one hundred and fifty miles, etc., and many of the feats performed by these dogs and dog drivers would be thought impossible to-day.

We were received very kindly by all parties, and I very soon felt at home with such men as R. Hardisty and Mr. MacDonald, and in the family of Mr. Flett where I received great hospitality, and from being a total stranger was soon made to feel thoroughly intimate.

I found that the Roman Catholics had a church built in the fort, and Mr. MacDonald and I went to the celebration of midnight mass on Christmas eve. Our conduct was respectful and reverent. Indeed, graceless as I may have been, I always from early boyhood have respected the religious services of others. Often in the conjurer's camp, and at thirst and sundances, I have preserved most perfect decorum and attention, and that night at Edmonton my friend and self behaved; but because someone saw MacDonald pass me a peppermint, it was noised abroad that we were mocking the passing of the wafer. Quite a furore was caused by this, and the Catholics came to the Chief Factor to demand our expulsion from the fort, but he very justly refused to interfere, and the storm passed away without hurting us. But I was amused and delighted with my friend, Mr. Woolsey. Said he to me, while drawing himself up and squaring off, "I never yet struck a man, but if I did, it would be a mighty blow."

Mr. Woolsey held service on Christmas morning, which was largely attended.

In the afternoon, Mr. Hardisty and myself went for a drive on the river with our dog-trains. Mr. Hardisty took the little daughter of the Chief Factor with him, and we drove up the river, but when turning to come home, his dogs took a sweep out into the river and left him, and the course the dogs took was dangerous. There was a long stretch of open current. There sat the child perfectly unconscious of her danger. Hardisty was winded, and he shouted to me to catch his dogs. I saw if I drove mine after his it would make matters worse, for his dogs would run the faster; so I left mine and ran after his, and here the constant training of the season did me good service. I had both wind and speed, but the time seemed dreadful. The dogs were nearing the current, and if the cariole should swing or upset, the child was doomed. If ever I ran, it was then; if ever I was thankful to be able to run, it was then. Little Mary was a favourite of mine, and her peril filled me with keen anguish; but I have always been thankful that my whole body responded as it did. Steadily I came up, and presently, before the dogs knew it, I was on the back of the sleigh; then, gripping the ground lashing, I let myself drag as a brake, and with a mighty "Chuh!" which made the leader jump quickly to the left, then a loud stern "Marse!" straight out from the danger the strong train drew us.

After we came home, I felt weak and exhausted because of the nervous strain; but the reward of having been instrumental in saving the little darling's life was sweet to me.

The next day we had dog-races, and footraces and football, and the fun was fast and furious. This social and pleasant intercourse with my fellowmen was especially agreeable to me after the isolation of the last few months. Then my new found friends were exceedingly kind, and I was heartily glad Mr. Woolsey had brought me with him to Edmonton.

At the Mission

A younger sister of the Rev. John McDougall, Eliza McDougall came from Ontario to Victoria mission in 1865, and there, at the age of sixteen, she experienced her first western Christmas. The missionary couple whom she so fondly mentions were her parents, the Rev. and Mrs. George McDougall. Victoria mission was located on the North Saskatchewan River about fifty miles northeast of Edmonton.

 might almost begin my story by "once upon a time," so long is it since my first Christmas in Alberta, forty-four years ago, [1865], at the little settlement of Victoria overlooking the Saskatchewan.

On Christmas Eve the snow had fallen covering the earth with a mantle of white, and the next morning when the sun broke forth, it shone brilliantly on the cluster of houses which formed the settlement, and on the mission house, and mission church on the outskirts, while across the river rose the fir clad banks of the Saskatchewan glistening in the sunshine. It seemed as if the world were singing for sheer joy, "Merry Christmas, Merry Christmas" while over the prairies rang the mission bell with its glad tidings, "Peace on Earth, Goodwill to men."

The mission church and schoolhouse combined was a log structure, whitewashed without, and boarded within, where everything was of the most primitive nature, though that day evergreens took away from the austerity of the room. Long wooden benches, without backs, seated the people, and at one end of the building a platform was erected from which the missionary looked down from the pulpit, built by the mission carpenter. It was a strange congregation that greeted him, Indians, half-breeds and whites. The year before a number of Red River half-breeds had followed him to settle down beside the mission that their children might be educated. They were there with their families. Among them sat a professor and his son, a squaw whose wrinkled face and drooping form told a story of deprivation and hardship, the prospector from the gold mine, an Indian brave in his war paint, and beside him his favorite wife and child, visitors from Hudson's Bay forts, Plain Crees, Wood Crees, all listening to the old story of the Christ child. There were some who heard it for the first time, and to all, I think, it came with a freshness and a new interest. Away out there on the

Facing page: This 1884 engraving, "Going to Church," shows a pioneer couple in the wilds of Canada.

28

prairies hundreds of miles from the nearest civilization, Christmas had not lost its old meaning.

The service over, "Merry Christmas, Merry Christmas" was heard on every side, and with many a handshake and good wishes, each departed to his own home.

Our Christmas would have seemed strange to many people. No Christmas tree, for there was nothing to put on it; no Christmas gifts, for there were none to buy, and nothing to make them of. Even the Christmas turkey was missing. Indeed it was difficult to get up a dinner one thousand miles away from the nearest town, no butcher, no baker, no grocer, all the people depended upon coming from St. Paul, Minnesota, or London, England. A bag of flour cost thirty dollars, and we had only two for that year, all the missionary could buy at Fort Garry the previous summer. White flour, indeed, was a luxury, kept for sickness, holidays, or Sundays, barley flour being used in its stead.

Buffalo meat, turnips, potatoes, plum pudding and barley cake — a novel Christmas dinner! But if the minds of the guests travelled back to more sumptuous feasts, the simple meal in no way lost by the comparison. For there were good appetites and grateful hearts for what was really a royal repast in those days, and throughout all was infused that spirit which alone makes a "Merry Christmas."

The mission house, like the church, was of logs, whitewashed without and boarded within, amply fortified against the severest winds. Down the centre of the dining-room was a long table, homemade, as were the chairs ranged around it. Bright pictures from magazines which had found their way across the continent from the Old Land decorated the walls, while buffalo robes strove to hide the bareness of the wooden floors. But best of all was the huge open fireplace with its blazing, crackling logs, the flames roaring up the wide chimney, defying Jack Frost, and crying "Merry Christmas, Merry Christmas" to the bright faces around the board.

It was a merry party. At the head of the table sat the missionary, still in the prime of life, his genial face beaming with the hospitality he loved to exercise, and, opposite him, at the far end of the long table, his pretty wife who had left all the comforts of the East to share in his great work, the christianizing of the North West. Besides their family of nine, four Hudson's Bay officers were spending the holidays with them, which was not only a welcome respite from the hardships of their lives, but which also added greatly to the enjoyment of the party.

After dinner came outdoor games, racing, throwing the hammer, tug-of-war, and football, not the football of today with its bitter rivalry, but governed by the spirit of good fellowship and played with all the zest of boys let loose from school, for life, a stern taskmaster to these men, granted them but little recreation. For did not their necessities and comforts depend on their own exertions? A buffalo hunt on the plains no doubt was good sport fraught with the danger all men love, but it also meant food and warmth for their families. They built their own homes, made their own furniture, hauled the great logs that glazed on their hearths, often plowed their

During the Christmas season of 1871, Charles Horetsky photographed the Rev. George McDougall family in front of their new Methodist mission at Fort Edmonton.

30

own fields, ground their own grain, and, at the same time, attended to their own particular line of work, that which had lured them from their Eastern homes.

Then came the sleigh drive. It was not a matter of going into a stable to harness a willing horse. Our drivers were in no one place, but scattered here and there round the mission, basking in the sunshine, playing at rough and tumble with one another, or barking at an occasional passerby. "Here Jumbo, here!" And Jumbo might obey. If not, then proceeded a chase and a scramble, and the unwilling dog was captured to be harnessed with his better behaved brothers.

When all was in readiness, the dogs were driven up to the door. The driver of each team stood on the back of his cariole, from which he commanded his dogs by word, not using the reins to guide them, but to hold them back if they were going too fast, or in case of his cariole being upset to keep the dogs from getting away, and so leaving him destitute on the prairie. The carioles were very much like a long box, lying flat on the snow, with the front curled up toboggan-like, and capable of holding one person.

As we came out of the house carrying our robes, well warmed beside the fire, the dogs were growing restless. How eager they were for the run, moving to one side, then to the other, their beaded blankets sparkling in the sun! Wrapped in our robes, and tucked cosily into our carioles, away we flew over the prairies. Jingle, jingle, jingle, went the bells, ringing out their music across the snow. Oh! the exhilaration of those old drives! Bright eyes, rosy cheeks, and the merriest laughter, uphill, down dale, through a fairyland of frosted trees — oh! those were the good old days!

A cry rang out, and turning we saw one of the carioles go over, the occupant an indiscriminate bundle of furs, and the driver, still holding the reins, being dragged through the snow. The dogs soon stopped, the cariole was righted, and the two unfortunates laughed out of all countenance. Then off we sped again on the home run, back to the welcome fireside, where fresh logs had been piled to greet our return.

When night fell, we found our way back to the little church, then lighted for a concert, which had been in preparation for several weeks, and in which the children, as well as the older members of the community, took part. Speeches were made, and songs were sung to the accompaniment of a little harmonium, the first musical instrument brought into the West, the West including Winnipeg, and bought by the missionary from Bishop Anderson, first Bishop of Rupert's Land. Stories were told of past Christmas days, bright pictures of happy times, but none there would really have bartered the merriest of them for that one which was then drawing to a close, and I know there are those still living who would gladly live it over again.

At last the day was ended, and the people wended their way homeward, some to the little settlement, others to their tepees on the plain, and the missionary with his family and guests to the mission house.

Christmas, 1872

Donald Graham, a young Scot, came to Manitoba during the Red River Rebellion of 1869-70, but after spending two years in the area, he decided to go buffalo hunting south of Fort Edmonton. It was his first Christmas out on the plains that he recalls in the following account. In later years he moved west to British Columbia and settled in the Okanagan valley.

hristmas in 1872 was not the day of days for us where comforts were concerned. There were no glittering electric lights nor colored tinsels to sparkle and glisten on the Christmas trees. No, but we had lots of towering Christmas trees sparkling with myriad diamonds, placed there by Jack Frost, who reigned as gloriously and triumphantly then as he does today.

Instead of the wonderful choirs singing beautiful Christmas carols, we would lie still at night and hear the howl of the wolves or the shrill cry of the coyote as he answered the call of his mate. And over all was the "Peace of the Plain." We seemed perhaps to understand better in those early days the true meaning of the words "Peace on Earth."

Perhaps the howl of the wolves would not seem like music to the ears of many today, nor take the place of the Christmas carols, but to me it had more of a thrill. Ever since my early days spent in the hills of Scotland I had longed for the time when I could roam over the plains and perhaps shoot a buffalo, of which I had read so much. So leaving Fort Edmonton early in December 1872, with my rifle and horse, dragging a long flat sled with some provisions and ammunition and tent material, I set out travelling south. Two companions joined me, one a Virginian [Addison McPherson], the other a Norwegian, known as "Dutch Charlie," [Charles Smith]. We travelled by easy stages, visiting with Indian tribes and pitching our tent when and where we felt like it.

After days of travelling, we reached some hills, I think now known as the Hand Hills. From the top of one of the hills we could see the prairie stretching for miles with hundreds of buffaloes feeding. What a thrill! Before we even had our lodge erected, I grabbed my rifle and started on the run. When I reached the place where I had seen the buffalo, there were plenty of tracks, but — no buffalo to be seen.

Next day, I said to my companions: "Is it true that tomorrow is Christmas day?"

"Sure thing, it's the 25th of December. What you think of doin? Hanging up your socks? Don't bother. There ain't no Santa Claus around here — no, nor turkey for dinner, neither."

"Well," says I, "I'm not looking for Santa Claus, but if I could only shoot a buffalo wouldn't a roast of that make a grand Christmas dinner?" "Sure would," said he, "but a greenhorn like you could never reach one. It takes the real Indians to do that."

There and then I made up my mind to get a buffalo or perish in the attempt. So taking my rifle, I set out. I could see from the top of a hill hundreds of buffalo feeding. There was timber on the north side of this hill, and suddenly I heard a crashing sound and turned just in time to see a huge buffalo coming on the run toward the hill where I was. I dropped out of sight until it disappeared in the hollow between the hills. I then ran until I reached a pile of brush. As I crouched there with my rifle cocked, it was only a minute or two till he passed me on the run just a few steps away — he looked as big as an elephant.

I shot him just behind the shoulder. He ran to the brow of the hill, then pitched forward on his breast, and slid right down the hill to the bottom. Was I proud? That was hardly the name for it. I was fairly dancing to think that I had really shot a buffalo. I did shoot many after that but none that ever gave me the thrill that I got from shooting this one.

After bleeding him and walking round and round before I could make up my mind to leave him, I hurried to our camp to tell the others. They came back with me, and after skinning it, we cut off the hind quarter and the tongue. Into the remainder I placed half a bottle of strychnine for the benefit of the wolves, which always followed a buffalo herd.

Next morning I was up bright and early, and visited what was left of the buffalo. There I found two dead wolves which we skinned, and Charlie cut out the back fat, a wide strip of which extended the full length of the back. As the strychnine never leaves the stomach, this fat is considered a great delicacy and was eaten with great relish.

And we did have such a merry Christmas dinner! We cooked the buffalo roast and ate it with bannocks made of flour and water and baked over hot stones — a feast fit for a king. After our dinner, we gathered around the camp fire, and Dutch Charlie told us stories of Christmas days and customs in Norway when he was a boy. The Virginian told us how they celebrated Christmas in Virginia, while I told of Christmas in Auld Scotland.

Since then I have spent many Christmas days in Alberta and watched the buffalo trails give way to ribbons of steel and highways filled with automobiles, and have seen the buffalo slowly but surely disappear from the prairie, but never have I spent a Christmas day so full of happiness and the joy of achievement as that first Christmas day so long ago, for had I not at last realized the joy of accomplishment and the fulfillment of one of my childhood dreams.

Christmas on the Plains

"Antelope Jim" McKernan was a member of the first North-West Mounted Police force, the one that marched west in 1874. Taking his discharge, he became a telegraph operator at Grizzly Bear Coulee, near the present Vermilion, Alberta, and it was from there that he set out on his Christmas adventure.

In the winter of 1877, my brother and I were living at a place called Grizzly Bear Coulee, about 130 miles west of Battleford, while far to the south of us there were two brothers who were old friends or acquaintances of ours, who had come up from Winnipeg in the late fall to trap, hunt buffalo, and trade with the Indians. It so happened that on their way west we met them and arranged that my brother and I should spend Christmas with them, if possible. To do this, it was necessary for me to leave Grizzly Bear on the 19th or 20th of December, so on the morning of the 20th we saddled our ponies, taking a third along as a pack horse and started south on the open plains to try and locate our two friends.

We were now right in the heart of the buffalo country, and as there was very little snow that winter, the buffalo had not gone south in any great numbers as it had been customary for them to do, so were very numerous. However, on the evening of the second day out we were beginning to think we were not going to locate our friends, but after camping for the night two-half-breed buffalo hunters came into our camp, and when we told them what we were after they explained to us (they both could speak English) that there were two tenderfeet boys camped at a small lake about 25 miles further on, and that we would have no trouble finding them. We were glad to get this information as we were sure it was the boys we were trying to find; then rolling ourselves in our blankets on the open prairie, we slept soundly till daylight.

After having breakfast, we saddled our horses for the last lap on our journey and reached our destination about two-thirty that afternoon. We found our friends in good health and glad to see us, but not any more glad than we were to be at our journey's end. They were camped in a small ravine close to a nice spring of fresh water and it was here we spent our Christmas on the plains, surrounded by hundreds, if not thousands, of buffalo and antelope.

Facing page: Fun is poked at a helpless English traveler caught in the Canadian wilds at Christmas. His guide offers him a rabbit for his holiday feast.

35

Christmas morning came clear and frosty, I should think about 10 or 15 below zero, and after breakfast it was decided that Tom, Bob and myself should go out for an antelope chase — buffalo being too easy to get — while Alf was left in camp to get our Christmas dinner. So we saddled our horses, examined our Winchesters to see that they were all in working order, mounted our horses, and headed for the plains, promising Alf that we would be back not later than four o'clock, and that we would expect something special for our Christmas dinner. In this we were not disappointed, for on our return after securing two antelope, we found a fine dinner of choice buffalo and antelope steak, together with an A1 plum duff and hot bannocks also a lot of other dishes on the side too numerous to mention, waiting for us.

Did you ever get a Christmas dinner ready at a camp fire, fair reader? Of course not. Well, it is no easy matter, but Alf made a success of it, and while we were turning our horses loose and hanging up the antelope, he had a fine spread on the grass, where we all seated ourselves and enjoyed as fine a dinner as I ever ate. Alf had thoughtfully arranged a fine camp fire which furnished sufficient heat to make things very comfortable.

Of course, after dinner speeches were out of the question as we had no booze, so we drank the health of the absent ones and the girls we had left behind, with a good cup of coffee, all standing around our camp fire. Tom, who was something of an orator, was called upon for a speech and although not very willing nevertheless said, "Well, friends, we four are here to-night in the wilds of the northwest, far from home and loved ones who no doubt have remembered us all today, but this is too sad and lonely a thought for us to be thinking about. Yet right here I wish to say that my brother and I have come out to this new country as pioneers to make our home, and I have no doubt but my two friends have done likewise. It is up to us all to brace up, mentally and physically, and enjoy the heritage that is in store for us. Let us put joy in our hearts and a tone of cheer on our lips, each doing his duty toward everyone and helping those who cannot help themselves. And may we all live to see this land a home for large numbers that may follow us. My brother and I wish our two friends a safe return to their little cabin at Grizzly Bear, and that we may enjoy many a happy Christmas in this new land." Thus ended my Christmas on the plains.

The Red River Settlement

Christmas at Red River Settlement

Joseph James ("J.J.") Hargraves was a son of the chief trader identified by Robert Ballantyne as "Mr. Grave" in his Christmas story. J.J. also served with the Hudson's Bay Company but was better known as the author of the book Red River, published in 1871. The Red River Settlement he describes was founded in 1811 on the banks of the Red River at the site of present-day Winnipeg. Like so many other settlers, Hargraves considered the community's "golden days" to have been during the 1860s, just before the West became a part of Canada.

uring the period of the existence of the colony at Red River previous to its adoption into the confederation of Canada, Christmas was the principal one of the few breaks in the monotony of its yearly life.

Occurring at mid-winter, it marked the passage of the shortest days and formed the turning point from which the earliest anticipations of approaching spring — still four months away — were dimly entertained. The winter tracks on river and plain, beaten by the traffic of a widely scattered and scanty population, would be getting into permanent trim, convenient for the passage of carrioles and cutters containing visitors on the way to visit relatives and acquaintances, often domiciled at considerable distances away.

An Englishman on his first arrival in the country would doubtless be inclined to view with dismay the vast plains over which the wintry wind whistled with unresisted sweep, and the bitter cold that compelled the traveller to bury himself in furs, mittens and caps protected with ear lappets, in order to escape from its inhospitable chill. On the other hand, the homes of the people were entirely exempt from poverty in its least endurable forms. Even the wandering Indian could always procure fuel for his wigwam fire, skins to cover him, and as a rule food to eat.

The Red River settlers were all in sufficiently comfortable circumstances and the Christmas week was for them a season of enjoyment after their fashion. Balls, frequently kept up for several successive days and nights, formed possibly the favorite diversion, at which the singular dance, known as the Red River jig, was the most invariably prominent feature. Strict sobriety was not a conspicious

Facing page: Some typical Christmas events in Manitoba are depicted in this 1881 illustration from the *London Graphic*.

One of the earliest advertisements for Christmas was published in *The Nor-Wester,* at the Red River Settlement, in 1864. It advertises a shipment of goods which had just arrived from Saint Paul.
Everything from clothing to tools were offered for sale or in exchange for hides or wool.

feature at these assemblages. Nevertheless, strangers in the country and travellers of experience in passing through it, found an interest in attending such gatherings and generally took both an active and lengthy part in the festivities.

With regard to table indulgencies, the numerous luxuries later imported in vast quantities were entirely absent. Fruits and the more perishable appendages of luxury were unknown. In later years, when capable of being preserved in cans, they were introduced, but by the 1860s this had not been attempted. The country itself, however, produced delicacies such as whitefish, venison and, above all, the buffalo with his flesh, his tongue, and his "boss" or hump.

At Christmas time, of course, all such good things were in special request and were supplemented by a class of stimulants, spiritous and vinous, excellent of their kind.

Absent friends were warmly remembered. This tendency was assisted by the fact that only a few days previously, say about the 15th of December, the dog trains bearing the packets of letters and postal matter for the northern districts and posts started from Fort Garry for Norway House. This was the opening stage of a vast and intricate system of intercommunication by means of which intelligence passed between every station belonging to the Hudson's Bay Company situated between the Rocky Mountains and Hudson Bay, and extending north to the Arctic Sea. Its extent and importance will be understood when it is remembered it was the only event of the kind occurring during the winter season. It was the winter mail of the Northern Department.

Everybody who could write made it a point to correspond with their friends by this opportunity, and hence the first fortnight of December was always a period of literary effort, the conclusion of which — as necessitated by the departure of the packet — left the mind relieved and ready to welcome the holiday season.

The packet system itself, as regards its aspect from Fort Garry, was so arranged that about the end of February the runners arrived, bringing out letters from the entire north, although, of course, only in cases of posts to the south of the river Saskatchewan could the latter be in reply to such as had gone out in December. In cases of the more northern posts, a letter would travel till almost spring before reaching its destination.

The arrival of these packet bearers was, of course, a great event at the interior posts. At Norway House, the first stage from Red River, the runners made it a point to pass their Christmas. This was found an arrangement as agreeable to them as to those who had for weeks been looking for them.

After the departure of the letters, the principal harbinger of the holidays, of a public character, was the celebration of Mass at midnight on Christmas Eve. This was always done at St. Boniface and, when possible, by Bishop Taché himself. It formed a very singular sight. The settlers, frequently from considerable distances, came driving in their carrioles by the magnificent winter moonlight night. The lighted windows of the cathedral, which was then an almost solitary building, gleamed on the surrounding snow and the

BRINGING HOME OUR CHRISTMAS STORES

The Back Log

Going to the Party

Morning Exercise

The Mail

A Smoking Party

music pealed impressively on the silent night. The solemnity was usually kept up until after 2 o'clock in the morning. Communicants were numerous and for many years perfect decorum was maintained. Latterly, however, this interesting ceremony was discontinued, I believe in a great measure because, in waiting for it, many persons were wont to find an occasion for conviviality which rendered their presence a source of disturbance to their more soberminded neighbors.

Ever since the establishment of the Church of England at Red River in 1820, Christmas day has been observed with religious worship. In the time of which I write, Divine Service was celebrated in the morning at St. John's Cathedral by the Bishop of Rupert's land, and was attended by the settlers at least as any of the weekly services of the church.

This is a view of the Saint Boniface cathedral in 1858.

Archbishop Taché Remembers

In 1882, Alexandre A. Taché, first Roman Catholic archbishop of Saint Boniface, was interviewed by a reporter from The Winnipeg Daily Sun, regarding his recollections of Christmases past.

y Christmas reminiscenses in the North-West for half a century!" laughingly exclaimed His Grace, the Archbishop of St. Boniface. "I should be delighted, but I'm not much more than half a century old myself, and I have only been in the North-West thirty-eight years. You can therefore see the inconvenience it would be to give you the reminiscences of fifty years.

"But you sit down and I will reply to such questions as you may ask.

"My first Christmas in the North-West?

"Yes, it was in 1845. There were then about fifteen houses in what is the Winnipeg of today. Some of them were comfortable dwellings. The other priests here at that time, besides myself, were Father Aubert and Father Lafleche, later the Bishop of Three Rivers, Quebec. The [St. Boniface] cathedral had two stone towers, with a tin belfrey. It was then in course of construction. There was nothing inside but the bare walls, and they were not even plastered.

"We held Midnight Mass; I remember it well. It was a beautiful, bright, clear, regular Manitoba night, with the thermometer down to 30 below. There were no stoves in the church and very few in the country. I also remember that some seven or eight panes of glass were broken, and there was no glass in the Great Lone Land to replace them. It was indeed a bitter, biting Christmas night, but notwithstanding this the church was crowded — yes, overcrowded. I think there were almost as many Protestants present as Catholics.

"A large number of those present came in sleighs. I should think there were 200 of them. Several of them were drawn by oxen. The people were very thinly clad. It was a mystery to me then, and has been ever since, how they stood the cold. I could see that they suffered a good deal during the service, as they kept moving their feet. But there was very little liquor in the country then, and people could stand the cold better.

"The Mass of that Christmas midnight was celebrated by Bishop Provencher, with Father Aubert as assistant priest, Father Lafleche

Archbishop Alexandre A. Taché.

41

"Return from Midnight Mass in Manitoba" is the title of this 1880 engraving.

as deacon, and myself, being the youngest, as sub-deacon. There was no organ in the church, but previous to the commencement of the service, Fathers Aubert and Lafleche entertained the congregation to a species of amateur concert on two clarionets, assisted by two half-breeds on violins. They played well, the people were delighted, and that was the first time that the music of clarionets and violins was heard in a church in the Great Lone Land.

"The Christmas carols were very sweetly sung by two Sisters of Charity — Sisters Lagrave and Gladu. Both had remarkably sweet voices. Notwithstanding the extreme cold, the open windows, and the absence of stoves, the service lasted over two hours. The exemplary behavior of the thousand people assembled evidenced their deep piety."

A Christmas Letter

An anonymous author described Christmas as enjoyed by the children of Red River Settlement in 1864.

ours past from this, the dear little ones below have been up and out of bed to ransack those stockings, puffed with comfits (declining, of course, the usual staple of breakfast, "just bread and butter.") They are now in the full tide of wonder and mutual display of their hordes of toys. Novices upon that noble animal, the "Rocking Horse," have ere this clasped wildly behind at his rigid tail, clutched madly in front at the flowing mane, and finally, with a yell of terror rolled from his back to look up and see the proud creature with his glass eyes blazing at nothing, continuing his untiring gallop as cool as his "Brummagen" stirrup iron. The creaking of ungreased wheels of barrows and waggons have resounded increasingly through the house, mingling with the blended din of mouth organs, cheap accordions, drums, whistles, trumpets, watchmen's rattles and such like incentives to harmony. Flutes and violins for the youngsters, whose mothers insist "have a perfect passion for music and such an ear," have been blown into, and scraped upon, until all the nervous dogs and cats in the neighborhood who haven't "a passion for music" have fled distractedly from the sound, leaving the tied-up "Towsers" to howl in dolorous unison.

Five times in every five minutes, has the new watch been held to the ear and opened "to look at the wheels"; once in every ten seconds have harmless coxcombs shoved beneath their eyes that "first pair of boots" and through all their talk and running and shouts and playing, the one hand has been deployed to dive incessantly into a deep pocket and fish out for the "munchers" overhead anything to be thought of from a sugar almond to a bit of "citron" stuck in and ornamented with broken pieces of almond shell on the one side and a mashed raisin on the other. Now have the new books been rushed through for the pictures and how does the big chap decide between two little ones, who are quarrelling as to which is Robinson Crusoe and which is man Friday.

Yes it is Christmas; it belongs to the children and sorrow lie at the door of him or her who would deprive them of their deep prerogative or darken with a word or look the sunshine in their bounding happy hearts.

Five years before his active role in the Red River Rebellion, politician John Christian Schultz was one of the first merchants to offer Christmas gifts for sale in the Red River Settlement.

The earliest known Christmas advertisement from the prairies appeared in *The Nor'Wester* at Red River on December 24, 1861.

How Riel's Prisoners Spent Christmas

In 1869, arrangements were made by the Dominion of Canada to take possession of Rupert's Land from Great Britain. This encompassed much of western Canada and included the Red River Settlement. However, the local people were not a party to the agreement and the Métis feared they would lose title to their land. When William McDougall was appointed lieutenant-governor of the new territory and tried to enter the region prematurely, the Métis rallied around Louis Riel and established their own provisional government. During the disputes which followed, a number of men were imprisoned while negotiations were held with Canadian authorities. In 1870, Canadian and British troops under General Garnet Wolseley arrived from Ontario, Riel fled, and the rebellion was over. The following account came from the pen of "An Old Resident."

When the morning of the 25th of December, 1869, came round in Red River, it found 63 prisoners in the hands of the Provisional Government of Assiniboia, of which Louis Riel was president.

They came to be there because when they were asked by a representative of Governor Macdougall to take up arms for their country they complied, but they soon found themselves deserted, and Riel finding them with arms in their hands, lodged them in jail.

He fed them with pemmican. It so happened that the Canadian Government owned some dozen or two quarters of beef. The writer, on applying for the use of this supply of meat, was allowed to use it as food for the prisoners. It could not be served raw and the only hotel in the place refused to cook it.

Fortunately, the representative referred to left behind him in the village a cooking stove, a man servant, a horse, and a leased house. The services of all were put in requisition and the wife of Brian Devlin, the only baker in the place, undertook for a consideration of five shillings, to bake a sack of flour, the flour being bought in the place.

In this way, it came about that every morning there was sent up to the prisoners two boilers full of hot tea and several loaves of bread, and every afternoon at about one o'clock, a mess of boiled beef and bread.

In 1869, Louis Riel and his Métis followers refused to permit William McDougall to enter western Canada to take up his post as lieutenant-governor. Instead, he camped at the international boundary until the rebellion was quelled. A humorist from the *Canadian Illustrated News* imagined the following conversation as McDougall celebrated Christmas in his tent while Indians threatened outside. "Hon. Mr. McD----l: Gentlemen, here we shall stay until we can advance with safety in to our own territory.
Mr. P-----r: Oh, M.l'Gouverneur! the only plan with safety is to go home!
Mr. B---g, (trying to warm his fingers, and practical withal), P----r, my dear friend, when will you pass me that flask?"

On the day before Christmas, the writer spoke to a few friends as to whether anything extra could be added to the very plain bill of fare on Christmas day.

All that could be done in the leased house would be the boiling of an extra quantity of meat and tea. Outside aid must be sought for the rest. George Emmerling, the owner of the hotel, professed himself willing to do what he could, but on referring to his better half was told that the dinner for their own guests would tax all their capacity.

At last, a promise of aid was cordially given by some ladies. In one house it was resolved a plum pudding should be made; a young lady, later the wife of a North-West magistrate, undertook the mysterious operation. Mrs. James Stewart lent a willing hand in the manufacture of pastry, and two o'clock the following day was fixed upon as the time at which all should be ready for despatch to the fort, nearly three-quarters of a mile distant.

The latter part of the repast came near being spoiled by the absence of dried fruit, which at last was obtained at eight o'clock in the evening at the store of Henry McKenney.

On account of the pressure of work at the leased house, it was found necessary to dispense with the usual breakfast. As no communication had been had with the prisoners as to the intentions of those outside, they unfortunately knew no reason for the absence of breakfast, and as the whole dinner was not ready until four in the afternoon, they had all come to the conclusion that for some unknown reason they were going to go without any outside food that day. Indeed, I believe many of them stayed their appetites with pemmican before our dinner reached them.

At four o'clock, however, Joseph Crowson, with his faithful black nag, was on his way with the beef, tea, pudding and pastry and, just as the darkness was settling down, he delivered his supplies to the starving prisoners.

It looked strange to see the sled on which the tea boiler was carried to the fort. The cover was not a good fit and the jolting of the sled caused the tea to run over the edge of the boiler, and in a few days a small mound of ice tea formed on the sled and daily received additions to its height.

The thanks of the prisoners were duly returned through Mr. Crowson to the ladies who had so kindly assisted to give relief to their otherwise monotonous fare.

This was the way, then, that they got their Christmas dinner.

Lower Fort Garry, at the confluence of the Red and Assiniboine rivers, held Louis Riel's prisoners during the Christmas of 1869.

A Dinner to Remember

When the Wolseley expedition traveled by steamer and on foot to Fort Garry in 1870, the men lived on a monotonous diet of salt pork, beans, and potatoes. On arriving in Manitoba and discovering Louis Riel's rebel forces had dispersed, they also learned that no supplies of fresh food awaited them. One person in particular who took the brunt of complaints was the quartermaster sergeant, whose duty it was to feed and satisfy twenty-five hungry men. After weeks of abuse, he finally served them a memorable Christmas meal.

t was the evening before Christmas, 1870.

On the ice of the Assiniboine, just below Fort Garry, the sporting men of the country were wont to speed their horses. The good quartermaster sergeant and Sergeant Hank wandered down to see the sport. The air was full of bell music and half-breed imprecations upon losing horses. The two good sergeants looked upon the merry scene and mechanically put up their big blanket shilling notes on the various likely horses. Suddenly something happened. Two horses, urged at full speed in opposite directions, collided. A shaft was plunged deep into the breast of one of the horses and he fell to the ice, kicked vigorously a little while, and died.

"There goes $500," said the owner. It is singular how much a killed horse is always worth. Ten minutes before the owner would have jumped at a $50 offer. The sport ended and the horsemen went home, leaving the carcass of the dead horse on the ice.

That evening, at supper, the sergeants growled their usual growl about the scarcity of fresh beef and the lavish plentitude of salt pig. They no longer dignified it by the name of pork.

The good quartermaster sergeant was again grieved. But the lines of care that excessive grief had brought to his handsome face were presently chased away by a broad grin — an inward sort of a laugh. He whispered to Sergeant Hank and they put on their great coats, muffled up and went out into the dark and frosty night.

Next day was Christmas.

Christmas day in barracks is the great day of the year. The sergeants made great preparations for the proper celebration of the day. The rooms were titified up and ornamented, and varnished, and fixed to no end. The wine list was appalling, and of spirits there were

47

The courtyard of Fort Garry is depicted here during the winter season.

more varieties than ever killed a man in the older provinces. The dinner was to be a great one. Many civilian friends had been invited to the banquet, and a most stupendous time was to be had.

"How about the dinner?" asked one hungry sergeant of the quartermaster sergeant. "Are you going to give us enough to eat today?"

Benevolence flickered all over the fine face of the Q.M.S. as he replied, "Yes, me boy; today you shall not grumble. Today's dinner will be one to be long remembered. Everybody will have everything they want, and all of it they want. Don't forget it!"

The dinner bugle sounded. The sergeants trooped in. My, what a spread! What a noble display of viands. What an astonishing variety. What a plentitude of everything. Beef! Beef everywhere. Beef soup, beef stewed, beef broiled, beef roasted, beef curried, beef a la everything, beef ad infinitum, beef galore!

They sat down. The face of the Q.M.S. beamed with pleasure. The good young fellow felt that, at last, he had distinguished himself. There was no longer any grumbling. Every eye shone with pleasure, every mouth watered with anticipation, and all showered compliments upon the bountiful Q.M.S.

"Pitch in, boys," shouted that personage. "What'll you have? Try the stewed beef. Is it good?"

"Good? Well, we should say so. Yum, yum. Betcherboots it's good," came from all sides of the table.

"Go to it, boys. How do you like the soup?"

"Haven't tasted anything half so good since I left Hamilton," said Staff Sergeant Jim as he helped himself to a juicy quarter section of roast beef.

Such a clatter of knives and forks. Such a disappearance of provender. Such uproarous laughter. Such jokes and quips, and such ejaculations of approval.

"Best roast beef I ever put a tooth in." "Capital curried beef that. Gimme more." "'Nother hunk off a that joint please."

It was a great feast and a long feast. It was the first opportunity the boys had had to make a good square meal since they left home. They said so, and they ate as if they spoke the truth. The beef was praised to the skies, and the good Q.M.S. was the most popular man in the regiment. At last the slowest — or greatest — eater had emptied his plate for the last time. All were satisfied. All looked supremely, superlatively, transcendently happy. The Q.M.S. saw his opportunity. He arose to his feet, smiled all around the board, and said;

"Gentlemen, have I satisfied you at last?"

Grand chorus: "You have."

"Is there one man here present who is not perfectly, absolutely satisfied?"

Grand chorus: "No, not one," and cheers.

"The dinner has been a great, a noble success?"

Grand chorus: "It has."

"And you would all like to have it repeated tomorrow?"

Members of the Wolseley expedition are seen crossing the ice of the Assiniboine River, with Fort Garry in the background. This event was sketched just after the expedition's Christmas festivities at the fort.

Rousing cheers and grand chorus, "We would."

The Q.M.S. turned to Sergeant Hank and said, "The best thing we can do, Hank, is to go down and get the rest of that old horse."

The sergeants looked blank for just two seconds. Then the situation dawned upon them. There were two doors to the dining room. In an instant both were crammed with anxious and escaping sergeants and civilians. They all had sudden and peremptory business outdoors. A man who passed that way about that time said it reminded him of the time he came across the ocean in an emigrant ship and struck the biggest storm that had blown for centuries.

Christmas, 1871

This poem, believed to have been written by Frank Larned Hunt, Manitoba's first lawyer, was published in The Manitoban, a Winnipeg newspaper.

Oh day of happiness, warm joys and friendly heat,
(Which Winter hard — at stern meridian — sets at naught),
Unheeding icy thralls the time it glows,
And sparkles with the radiance of the gemming frost,
Whose cunning hand has wove the festal pictures,
That greet the kindly holy day,
And draws for prince and cottager alike
A wizard curtain to the outer world.

Clear, bracing strung with very glee doth seem the air,
The crisp snow crackles to the springy foot,
And gifts the stealthy moccasin with sound.
The hearty rigor of the days — the cold, the happy days,
Awakes the current of the tranquil blood
Which hurries from the gladsome cheerful heart,
To post beneath her sentinels, the eyes, and ruddy glows defiant,
As with a laugh the eager blast doth buffet speed and flee away.

Cheer, heartsome cheer! and rings the unspoke benison,
Hope, Heavenly Hope — doth seem to breathe — this is
my natal morn.
The mind doth teem with Christmas Hymns — sweet as the day;
And beams the earth with gladness love and praise;
The myriad accord which nations sing,
Hail Prince of Peace, Redeemer, Lord and King!

The Mounted Police
My Darling Liz

Richard Barrington Nevitt was a young medical graduate in Toronto when in 1874, he signed up as assistant surgeon in the North-West Mounted Police. Promising his girl friend, Elizabeth Beaty, that he would return after four years of service, he set out on the great march from Manitoba to southern Alberta, where Fort Macleod was erected. This letter to Elizabeth describes his first Christmas at the fort. True to his word, Nevitt later went back to Toronto and married the girl.

Fort Macleod, N.W.T.
December 27th, 1874

 y darling Liz
It seems such a time since I have written to you, but it cannot be very long for your letter has not gone yet. It was the 24th, Thursday, that I finished it, and in a great hurry I was too.

After lunch on the 24th I got [Inspector] Denny to come with me and we went down through the bush towards Kanouse's, both with rifles. I saw four fine deer but did not get a shot at them. We went a long, long way and at last saw some more deer far off from the immediate bank of the river, feeding on the hill side as it slopes down from the prairie to the river bottom. We made a wide detour and climbed the steep hill and out on the prairie level and crept towards the deer. We got above them and figuring to try and get near fired at a long range and missed them. There were six of them; we were very much disgusted and came home. We got into camp just as the bugle sounded the "Dress" for dinner. Our dinner was very nice, the table laid with a sheet as a tablecloth. It is the only sheet in camp. After dinner I went to my room and with Ferland, my Hospt. Sergt., began to dissect some eyes of a deer. I finished them during the evening altho' I was interrupted by various calls as Secretary of the Mess Committee.

Christmas day, of course, was observed as a Holyday. In the morning Capt. Jackson fired off our big gun with shells at an old tree and struck a branch of it, cutting it off completely. The pow-wow that was to have taken place the day before was put off on account of all the Indians not being able to get there. Instead we are to have it on Christmas. All the morning men were busy making mottoes to be hung around the room. They were painted in vermillion on white cloth and looked very well. "The Nor'West Mounted Police, Pioneers of a Glorious Future," "Law and Order is Peace and Prosperity," "Our Absent Friends, God Bless 'em." How my heart echoed back "God Bless them." How I wondered then what you were doing and where you were. I knew wherever you were and whatever you were doing you would think of me, did you not, old woman? I know you did, but I want to hear you say you did. How I would like to see you and hear you speak, fold you in my arms once again. Oh Liz when I come back we won't separate again for so long, will we? I don't think I could be happy after seeing you again, to leave you for so long.

At two o'clock the Indians came and we took them out on the prairie to show them the effect of our artillery at a long range. They were greatly impressed thereat and after returning to the Mess Room we proceeded to feed them, Biscuit, Rice & Molasses & Coffee. They ate until they were portly full and then the Col. [Asst. Commisioner James F. Macleod], taking the Chiefs aside, talked to them. The squaws came and had a show in the good things going; some of them were quite handsome for squaws but all of them dirty. The young "Bucks" were all dressed to kill — feathers and paint and furs and gaudy blankets and beads. They all went away quietly about 5 o'clock. The men of the Troops had invited their respective Officers to dinner at their quarters in the middle of the day and from what we can hear they had most sumptuous repasts. Our dinner was not to be despised as the enclosed "Bill of Fare" will show you. The last course finished, we had a small jar of whiskey brought on the table, a present from [Fort] Benton, and in whiskey we drank to our "Absent Friends". No other toast was drunk and no speech was made, for none was required. Then sitting round the table smoking, we talked of Christmases gone by, of friends & home.

About eleven o'clock we went over to "B" Troop to a dance and concert given by the men. Some of the songs were excellent, the dancing quite enjoyable and the remainder of the evening passed in revelry. About 12 we went to "F" Troop for supper and there had oysters, canned fruit pies, rice pudding, plum pudding and lots of it. The Interpreter then sent for the squaws and at 2 o'clock they came over and danced. We gave them some supper and 4 o'clock saw the end of the Christmas Day.

I guarantee that such a Christmas had never been seen in the Nor'West. Everyone expected to have a gloomy sad time, but the united efforts of men and officers managed to dispel the gloom and if Christmas was not exactly merry, it was at all events, pleasant.

Your own,
Barrie

Menu for the officers' mess at
Fort Macleod, Christmas, 1874.

Tragedy at Fort Macleod

Cecil Denny was one of the original officers of the North-West Mounted Police and later became Sir Cecil, the Sixth Baronet of Tralee Castle in Ireland. While Doctor Nevitt in his account recalls the pleasures of his first Christmas at Fort Macleod, Denny tells of a tragedy which occurred just after the doctor had written to Liz.

small police detachment was stationed some eighteen miles [from Fort Macleod], down the Old Man's River at an abandoned liquor trading post, named Fort Kipp after the original builder. It was the customary log structure, surrounded by a stockade. An officer named Brisebois was in command. Two of his men had spent Christmas on leave at Fort Macleod; they left to return to Kipp two days before New Year. On that day word was brought to the fort that a Baker Company bull team, loaded with supplies and mail for us, had arrived at Whoop-up [near the present Lethbridge], but would be at least a week in reaching Macleod. We naturally were most anxious to get this mail at once, since no letters or papers had reached us since leaving Dufferin [Manitoba] in June; particularly we wished to have it by New Year. I therefore asked permission of Colonel Macleod to ride to Whoop-up, pick up the letters, and return by that time.

The colonel hesitated, but being himself anxious to hear from the Commissioner, he at last consented. I started on the evening of 31st December, riding a tough little Indian pony, with the intention of staying overnight with the detachment at Kipp and returning to Macleod the following day. Snow on the ground made the trail faint. I had made about half the distance when a sudden change of the wind, bringing a north-west blizzard, decided me to turn back. The temperature fell to twenty degrees below zero, I found it impossible to make headway with the wind and snow full in my face, and I had difficulty in keeping my eyelids from freezing together. The slight trail was soon blotted out. I had no alternative but to turn my back to the storm and trust to the horse to find the way to Fort Kipp. Luckily I was wearing a warm buffalo coat, but even this and my buffalo skin moccasins did not prevent me suffering considerably, and I only saved myself from freezing by dismounting at intervals and running beside the horse. In doing so, however, I was in danger

The Christmas season of 1874-75 was a tragic one for two Mounted Policeman who lost their way traveling to Fort Kipp, above.

of leading the horse away from the point for which he was making. I could see only a few yards in any direction through the blizzard.

Darkness came on, and I did not dare leave the saddle, to the pommel of which I fastened the reins, letting the horse have his head. Fortunately he had been bred in the vicinity and was wonderfully intelligent; he never went out of a walk, but kept plodding long hour after hour through the storm. Around midnight it cleared somewhat, and I could see dimly ahead what I took for the steep bank of the river. I trusted to the horse and he plodded on. The storm thickened again, and for another hour nothing was visible.

Then suddenly I found myself surrounded by lighted windows. Without my realizing it the horse had walked through the open gate of Fort Kipp and stopped in the middle of the square. It was fortunate I had put my trust in his intelligence; otherwise we should no doubt have been lost, and I would have perished.

Fort Kipp that night was a welcome haven. The comfortable rooms, with their blazing log fires and a warm meal, soon put my blood again in circulation. I inquired of Inspector Brisebois if the two men, Baxter and Wilson, who had been in Macleod on leave, had returned. His reply being that he had not seen them, we concluded they had taken shelter at a small trading post some ten miles up the river, and would come in the following day.

Next morning was clear and I rode to Whoop-up, returning to Kipp in the afternoon with the letters. Here I learned that the horses ridden by the missing men had come into the fort, riderless, soon after I had left, and a party accompanied by Indians had been sent out to search for them. Just before I started for Macleod the poor fellows were brought in, one frozen stiff, the other, Wilson, still breathing, but with arms, legs, and most of his body frozen also. I took a fresh horse and rode as fast as the snow would allow to Macleod, and on my reaching there Dr. Nevitt raced to Fort Kipp, only to find on arrival poor Wilson dead.

The search party had followed the trail of the unfortunate men's horses to where they had wandered in a circle, and then laid down, soon to freeze in that bitter north wind. Shortly after this sad occurrence another man named Parks, ill from the exposure and hardship of the march, died in the rude hospital at the Fort. These three deaths cast a gloom over us all, and our first New Year in the West. The bodies of Baxter and Wilson were brought to Fort Macleod and buried with military honours by their comrades, with whom they were great favourites.

Christmas at Swan River

The author, William Parker, was another of the original members of the North-West Mounted Police. During the Christmas season in 1875, he was stationed at Swan River Barracks, 250 miles north-west of Winnipeg. At that time, everyone believed that Swan River would become the permanent capital of the North-West Territories and headquarters for the police. However, this later proved to be impractical. Just after Christmas, 1875, Parker wrote to his mother in England, telling her of the festive season.

he last mail arrived here at a most appropriate time, just three days before Xmas. Directly the mail was seen coming through the gate, there was a general rush made for it, the dogs were caressed, and called most affectionate names for coming through in such good time, a hundred and forty miles in two days. Being Xmas there was a large mail. I was one of the most lucky ones, received seven letters. Perhaps you can imagine how lively I dived into their contents. Yours were the first, there were three, one enclosed by Harry, and two swell ones straight from yourself, one from dear Father which was very interesting, one from Harry who did not injure himself by writing too much, one from old Tadpole, telling me of the splendid times he enjoyed at St. Mary and he thinks he would like to become a "Buck Policeman". The last was from my kind friend Mrs. Almon at Dufferin; she says the weather there is most disgraceful, forty below zero when she was writing.

We have been having a very Merry Xmas. In the first place we decorated the room, which I assure you looks really beautiful and would do credit to any civilized country. In one end facing the door is an evergreen arch, with a Merry Xmas on it in large red letters, underneath is a crown with two small Union Jacks on each side under that again are two carbines crossed and two Royal Standards on each side, with a star of ramrods between, and at the bottom of all, our best friend in need, the Babcock Fire engine polished up very bright. At the opposite end, another arch with a Happy New Year on it, and underneath, God Save the Queen, in evergreen letters made by myself in the old St. Mary's style. I must say, though I shouldn't, they were much admired by the fair sex. The three pillars in the centre were covered with evergreens, and all along the centre of the ceiling there were wreaths all round the room, and on the walls between each window a ring of evergreen with two carbines crossed over them and two revolvers crossed inside the ring. In each window hung a sort of birdcage made of evergreens with a candle burning in the centre. There were three evergreen chandeliers hanging up in the centre of the room.

But the dinner was the main thing, three tables struggling under the weight of good things of every description. It would take up too much time and room to name them all, nevertheless I can give you a little insight into the matter. There were four hundred and fifty pounds of Roast beef, the choicest joints, rabbits cooked in about sixteen different ways, prairie chickens and partridges, mutton hot, mutton cold, seven cold hams. The pastry composed of sixty pounds of plum pudding, fifty-four pies of every kind of canned fruit, such as gooseberries, peaches and strawberries. After all this came soothing jellies of different varieties, almonds and raisins and plates piled high with candies or rather sweets. But there was something we missed greatly and that was a wee glass of wine. Coffee and tea were poor substitutes at Xmas time.

After dinner was over and we had had an hour's breathing, the pleasures of the evening commenced. Amongst the visitors were Col and Mrs. French, Col Griffiths and his two fair daughters, two Sub Constables' wives and all the officers; we all enjoyed ourselves thoroughly. One of our Sub Constables, who has been an old lawyer in his time, took the chair and he fulfilled his position bully. I was called upon to open the proceedings with a song which I did by singing the Roast Beef of Old England, it took immensely. Then the speeches and toasting commenced. Some of the speeches were bully and there was great laughter. The toasts were given by three lusty cheers. The dear ones at home seemed to get the loudest cheer. We were complimented greatly on our decorations; there were some splendid songs sung and some very good singers amongst us, although I cannot sing worth a cent. The proceedings broke up about twelve o'clock after thoroughly enjoying ourselves. There was also a shooting match between the officers; the Canadian officers came out victorious.

We are now very busy preparing to meet the New Year. There is to be a dance and grand shooting match between English, Scotch, Irish, and Canadians; it is looked forward to with great interest and will be hotly contested, five men to represent each nation. We were practising today. I did pretty good, came out second best.

I am afraid you will think your son Bill a course 'un when he comes home; never mind I will try my best to please you.

Christmas at Fort Calgarry

A Mounted Policeman, identified only as "S", wrote to the Toronto Mail to tell how Christmas had been celebrated at Fort "Calgarry" in 1877. The letter, sent by courier to Fort Benton, Montana, was affixed with American postage stamps and carried the return address: "Fort Calgarry, Montana, U.S."

 t may not be amiss to inform you of what we are doing at this post during the festive season just closed and to let you see that although buried in the wilderness, and cut off from all social intercourse with our white fellow men, we still manage to eke out a not intolerable existence, and when excuse offers a good time of it.

F Division, stationed at Fort Calgarry, commemorated Christmas by a troop dinner, given in the mess room, which was most tastefully decorated with evergreens, flags, and mottoes suitable to the day, the chair being occupied by Captain Crozier, our commanding officer, whose recent appointment has given universal and solid satisfaction to his subordinates. He is no stranger to many of his men, having already had the troop command, at a most trying time, that of their great march from Dufferin, and a hearty welcome awaited his return to it.

The dinner itself was capital and, for the time being, made all forgetful of their isolated lot; in fact, it was hard to believe they were

The first Christmas celebrated by the Mounted Police at Fort Calgary was in 1875. The building had just been completed, as seen in this painting rendered a few weeks after the festive season. At that time, Calgary was an isolated outpost in the wilderness.

dining within forty miles of the Rocky Mountains, and in a country where earthern floors are the rule, and carpets, staircases, wine and beer luxuries are unknown, though not undreamed of — especially the latter. Lord! how we thirst for it sometimes!

The whole country round were invited for the evening, the inducements being theatricals and songs, followed by a dance, the highest pinnacle of a half-breed's enjoyment. The plays were

57

Facing page: Christmas card of the Battleford detachment of the Mounted Police, 1911.

specially written for the occasion by Westwood "of ours," and were a decided success, due as much to their dashing conception as to their dramatic talent shown in the parts. There is now almost a certainty of a good amateur club being formed, the only trouble being, that not having books, we shall have to invent our plays as we go on. Perhaps all the more fun on this account. The plays were followed by songs, then came the dance. It was an interesting picture, the gaily decorated room garnished with squatting women and children (for whole families came, down even to the last arrival), fiddles going, lights flaring, and in the centre, dancers performing feats of agility as indescribable as they are impossible for a white man to imitate. Refreshments, or rather a substantial supper, disappeared about midnight, and, with renewed spirit, quadrilles, jigs, and nondescript figures were kept up until nearly reveille.

This was the last Christmas dinner many of the troop will eat together, as early next spring two-thirds of the men will return to civilian life, their term of service being up. Most of them will go back to Canada, blessing their stars at getting safely out of this worthless waste — only to return again to it, so alluring are the charms of a prairie life.

Christmas Greetings

These verses were first published by the Macleod Gazette in 1882.

A greeting my readers I give unto all,
Into whose hands this paper chances to fall.
A greeting which often our fair hearts doth cheer,
'Tis "A Merry Christmas and Happy New Year."

Be you Yankee, Canadian, or Half-breed free,
Police officer, Policeman, or Eastern M.P.,
Cattle king or cowboy, I care not a jot;
Or a swell from the Old Country fresh and hot.

To each one and all I at this time extend,
This welcome of friendship to all as a friend.
Old settlers, noted as "wrestlers" bold,
Have learned in the past how to gather up gold,

But whilst all here strive for what most men still crave,
In the hour of death its man's soul cannot save.
There's a pearl of great price offered free to all,
Which this Christmas season to our minds recall;

Let all then take heed this great pearl first to find,
To which the world's wealth is not equal combined.
It is offered alike to rich and to poor,
And upon the holder will always ensure,

In the midst of this world its toil and its strife,
In the pressure of business and bustle of life,
In sickness, in health, a true friend ever near,
With "A Merry Christmas and Happy New Year."

Cricket at Christmas

C.E.D. Wood, editor of The Macleod Gazette, wrote this editorial in 1885, as much for his eastern subscribers as for local residents.

e venture to say that in no part of the Dominion, except in the extreme west, was it possible to play cricket on Xmas Eve. And yet Major Cotton and others did play on that day, and all unite in saying that it was the most perfect cricketing weather. Think of this, ye ice-bound people of Ontario and Quebec. Look out of your windows at the snow and ice piled up around you; just gaze on your solid rivers; wrap yourselves up warmly lest you freeze — and then rivet your attention on the land over which the Rocky Mountains look. Just picture to yourselves clear sunshiny days with the thermometer up in the fifties; no ice and snow to make one shiver and shake; the rivers running as if it were August; men wearing their summer clothes. Think of all this and weep. Lift up your voices and lament that you cannot live in God's country, where the greatest stretch of winter weather is six weeks or two months, and sometimes there is none at all; where a cold day is seldom followed by another, and the farmers can plough in January and February. Frigid, arctic Ontario! Tropical North-West! What a contrast, and what an utter falling-to-pieces of the old time fallacy that the North-West was as near the North Pole as it was possible to get.

Indian Reserves

Celebrating the "Big Holy Day"

The Rev. John W. Tims was the Anglican clergyman who established Saint John's mission on the Blackfoot Reserve south of Gleichen, Alberta in 1883. A short time later he opened a boarding school, which developed into the Old Sun Indian Residential School. In this article, he recalls mission-school Christmases in the 1880s and traces them through to the 1920s.

san-is-tsis ak-o-to Omuk-a-to-yi-ksis-tsi-ku-yi?"
"When will the Big Holy Day arrive?"
A month or six weeks before Christmas this is the question uppermost in the minds of the Indians and addressed almost daily to those whose lot is cast among them.

Being a Christian festival, it was unknown among the Blackfoot-speaking people fifty years ago, but it has gained such a hold upon them that they now look forward to it as much or more than they do to the Calgary Stampede.

The writer remembers the difficulty he had in the early days in trying to make them understand the meaning of Christmas. When, with but an imperfect knowledge of their language, he told them through an interpreter that "God sent His Son into the world," the interpreter, whose grasp of English was equally poor, told them that "God sent *Natos,* the sun, into the world."

But the Indians realized that the day had some special meaning to the white man when they were all called together to a feast and distribution of clothing in the little log school building. It took a day and a night to prepare for the affair. Bales of clothing had arrived from England, consisting of warm garments for men, women and children. This had to be sorted out in the Mission House the day previous, with blinds drawn, for swarthy faces would be pressed close to the window-panes with blankets drawn up over the heads to see whatever might be seen.

The whole night was spent in boiling beef and cutting up bread and then slicing the meat to make sandwiches and finally preparing a boiler full of good, black tea. At one such feast the greatest amusement, which might well have been otherwise but for the fun it aroused, was caused when by mistake a five pound package of Epsom salts was used instead of a similar quantity of sugar to mix with the tea. Packets of each were in the cupboard done up in brown paper as they had been brought back from the store, and the wrong one had been taken. The error was only discovered when some of the Indians began to ask for a further supply of *Is-tsi-ksi-pok-ko,* salt water! When the joke was explained to them they seemed to enjoy it, but it helped to shorten the party, for soon one by one everybody made for the door, and the distributor was left alone.

At ten o'clock in the morning the chief was told that all was ready, and according to Indian custom he walked through the camp crying, *"Ni-nau-uk, a-ke-u-uk, po-kau-uk, O-muka-is-sto-wan kit-um-mok-o-au."* "Men, women, children, Big Knife invites you to the feast!" And the camp was alive with a great throng of human beings of all ages, with faces painted all colors, with bodies clothed in flour sacks, striped demin, Hudson's Bay blankets or old buffalo robes, and decorated with earrings and necklaces, with bracelets on their arms and rings on almost every finger of both hands and composed chiefly of brass and copper wire twisted round in several strands.

The tea, food, and clothing had already been carried into the school room and placed at the far end of the building. When the door was thrown open the people poured in in one long stream. There were a few seats along the walls. These were soon filled by some of the leading men. The women and children squatted on the floor and as the Indians continued to stream in there was such a crush that they were like herrings packed in a barrel.

How to reach the people with the sandwiches was a problem. They had to be passed along from hand to hand, and the tea in the same way. There was no need for crockery of any description. The food was taken in the hand. The Indians all brought their own utensils for the tea. And what a variety of utensils there were! There were old wooden basins of native manufacture, tin cans holding half a gallon, and toilet articles of every description. Details must be left to the reader's imagination. The women carried under their blankets small sacks in which they deposited all the food and candies that the family could not eat, and large cans into which all the tea was collected. There was certainly nothing wasted.

The food having been all consumed, the next thing was the distribution of the clothing — shirts, mufflers or socks for the men, flannel petticoats or woolen crossovers for the women, warm dresses for the girls, and shirts, socks and woolen helmets for the boys.

The building at once became one mixed dressing room. The men and boys commenced to adorn themselves with their shirts, the women stepped into their petticoats, the girls into their dresses, and both boys and men left the school with their shirt tails flowing in the breeze, for having no trousers, only breechclouts and leggings, all of the shirt had to remain visible. Before they left, however, the children were all called upon to sing in their native tongue a translation of "O come, all ye faithful," which had been taught them in school.

The poverty of the Indians in those days, when the annuity from the government of $5.00 per head was about all the money they could look forward to, and the rations doled out to them were the meagerest, made them only too grateful for the clothing which the missionary was able to hand out to them. The English bale was soon augmented by new and second hand clothing from the Women's Auxiliary of the church in eastern Canada.

Waistcosts were a much-prized article of clothing in those days, for the little pockets were found so useful in which to carry the ration tickets which had to be shown twice a week when going for the beef and flour. On one occasion a man became so angry because there were not enough to go round that he seized the missionary and demanded the waistcoat he was wearing — but he didn't get it.

On another Indian reserve, in addition to useful wearing apparel, several women's hats were sent up in the bale. One was a straw with

Archdeacon J. W. Tims, center, recalled his early Christmases with the Blackfoot Indians. He is seen here with some of his new students about 1890 before their hair was cut and their blanket coats exchanged for grey uniforms. With Tims are the Reverend J. W. Haynes and Miss Brown.

a large feather which especially attracted the men. The missionary was mobbed by a number of the Indians in their desire to become its proud owner. The man into whose possession it came only retained it for a few minutes before he disposed of it to another in exchange for a cayuse!

As time passed and the system of residential schools was established, the Christmas feast became a more orderly affair. The Indians were admitted in batches and were served the meal in the dining room, sitting up to tables provided with enamelware plates and mugs. The bread and meat was supplemented with apple pie or other dessert. The women still brought their small sacks and cans under their blankets to carry away all that they or their families could not eat. It was often a wonder to a new worker that the Indians were able to get away with such quantities of food and tea, until the receptacles under the women's blankets were pointed out to them.

The years went on, and as the teaching given in the schools and in the churches, which had now been erected for their use, began to be better understood, the real spirit of Christmas seemed to take possession of them. The Christmas service became the chief thing on that morning. The Indians arrived early in order to see their children in the residential school, and to bring them presents before the hour of service. The church was packed with worshippers who joined in the singing and prayers as heartily as a white congregation, and the offerings were quite equal in proportion to those in the white churches.

As means of obtaining a livelihood opened up, the gifts of clothing gradually ceased, for they were able to purchase all they needed from their own earnings. They still have a feast on a day during the festival week, when they are invited with their children to the school, and attend the concert or entertainment provided by their boys and girls.

But the Indians are not satisfied with that. They must now make feasts in their own homes. For this they work hard for weeks previous to Christmas. They go to the bush to cut dry wood and haul it into the city for sale. They drive for miles to locate and haul fir trees into town — all for this one purpose, that they may make a good feast and be able to invite all their friends.

The great change that has come over the Indians in this part of the country is inconceivable. The writer has been invited of late years to the annual feast given by Chief Joe Big Plume on the Sarcee Reserve. China cups and saucers for the tea, china plates for the food, which consists largely of canned stuff, fruit, nuts and candy, to say nothing of the pies and cakes that his wife and some of her friends have spent most of the previous night in preparing. All this is set out on long tables put up for the occasion. The people come in and sit down, as many as can do so at one sitting. When they have finished, another lot takes their place, a number of young women the meanwhile clearing the tables and washing up the used crockery. In the evening all adjourn to the council hall and wind up the day with an old fashioned dance.

By the first of the New Year, the Indians will be as poor as they were before they began to sell firewood and Christmas trees. But somehow they will find a way of providing for themselves and their dependents during the remainder of the winter.

From a Blackfoot Boy

In 1894, a teacher helped a Blackfoot Indian student to write this letter to the editor of the Calgary Herald. He signed himself as Sokumapi, which is the Blackfoot word for "boy."

ou have been telling in your paper of the way all the white people enjoyed themselves at Christmas and New Year, so now please let us tell you how we enjoyed ourselves on the Blackfoot reserve. Well, to begin with, we boys and girls take a great interest in Santa Claus and as he paid us a visit last year, we thought we would get something again, so we got a long rope and stretched it across the room and put all our stockings and socks on it on Christmas eve. He came sure, and we all got candies and nuts and plums and one boy got a card sent from England and the girls got scissors and hair ribbons too.

At 11 o'clock on Christmas Day we had service in our new schoolhouse and heard about Jesus being born and sang our Christmas hymns in Blackfoot. At 1 o'clock, O my! we had a fine dinner, roast beef and plum pudding. Three big plum puddings, one for each table, and Albert, he couldn't eat his all up, and Mr. Tims, he said it was the first time Albert said he couldn't eat any more.

Well, after dinner we went on to the ice to play and at 5 o'clock the big bell began to ring and there was no boy late for tea this night. We never saw anything like it before. The cakes were all white on the top and little rabbits and mice all over them, but the boys soon found it was all sugar, and there were no rabbits or mice after tea. Well, when tea was over we heard a great noise, and the boys, they said it was old Santa Claus come, and we all ran out and there he was coming over from the Mission house with a long white beard, and a dress like an old woman, and a bundle of things on his arm and we all laughed at him and we all went into the school house. Then we saw what Mr. Baker and Miss Garlick and the other teacher had been doing all the afternoon. They had got a pine tree and dressed it up with all sorts of things, and all the boys and girls looked happy.

Old Santa Claus, he said some of the Indians could come in and see it too, so a lot of our fathers and mothers, they came in and sat down and the tree was lit up with candles and Santa Claus began to give us some things. The boys got boots, braces, handkerchiefs,

HERE'RE MY PRESENTS.   AND MINE.

Medicine Hat News,
December 20, 1894.

knives, and the little boys got tin horses and dogs and the girls they got dolls and work bags and one got a knife, fork and spoon in a box all the way from Toronto. Then we had apples and scrambled for nuts and candies which Santa Claus said Mr. Haynes sent.

After that we had games and played "nuts and may" and "turn the trencher" and all the Indians, they played too, and we sang songs and that was how we spent Christmas.

Very good, sir. And then at New Year, Mr. Tims always gives our parents a feast then and about fifty Indians all came to the school-house and had bread and beef, and apple pies, and lots of tea, and Mr. Tims he gave to each father a quilt and a shirt or coat or something that came up in the bales, and our mothers (some of us have 2 or 3 mothers) they had a dress or a petticoat and something else, a hood or a scarf. This was the parents' feast. Then the next day all the other Indians came, and the children got something, a pair of mitts or a doll and Mr. Tims he gave all the old women petticoats or something else and the girls got dresses and the boys scarfs and hats and everybody had tea and bread and jam and all we boys and girls had candies.

I don't know how many people there were, about 150 I should think. This was all New Year's at this camp. Eagle Ribs' people at the South Camp, where there is another school, they had New Year's too and got some things same as the Indians here. Next year, Mr. Editor, I will tell you again what we do, and I hope there will be a lot more bales [of clothing] come up again.

Christmas Day

Mike Mountain Horse was a Blood Indian who was enrolled in Saint Paul's Anglican mission, southeast of Fort Macleod, in 1894. After graduation he served overseas during World War I and went on to become the author of Indian stories. In this account, he recalls various Christmases, including one at the home of his father-in-law, Joe Healy.

n those early days [1890s] Christmas services were held in log huts on the Blood Reserve. Any available hut was utilized by these early missionaries for this purpose. Their congregations consisted mostly of men who squatted on their varied colored blankets on the earthen floor. A few women also attended. We children, almost naked, would make ourselves a nuisance by continually running back and forth to the hut where the service was being held. Scores of skinny, mangey mongrels of all descriptions would also converge at the place of worship. Frequently these latter would start a fight among themselves causing a great deal of excitement among the children who would try to separate their pets from the other combatants. Our parents' main reason for bringing their children to hear the "Holy White Man," as they called him, was the supply of hard candy which was distributed to us at the close of the service. He would also invite our parents to his little home and hand out clothes such as coats, scarves, mitts, and various other useful items, as Christmas presents.

About the only Indian of our tribe who celebrated Yuletide in his home at that time was Joe Healy. He also had an "at home" for the Indians in general. Everybody was welcome at these gatherings. Great preparations were made for this special day when Flying Chief — as he was called — was going to feed his friends. From early morning to late at night wagons loaded with Indians, men, women and children, would be seen driving from all parts of the reserve toward Healy's house, numerous dogs following in their wake. A few men rode horseback, while an occasional woman might be observed, with her papoose sitting contentedly in a travois which her mount was carrying. Any Indians whose cabins were in close proximity to Joe's house arrived on foot to enjoy the hospitality of Mr. Healy and his good wife. A long table laden with juicy roasts, vegetables of all

JOS. HEALY - WOLF MOCCASSIN FAMILY

Mike Mountain Horse recalled the Christmas feasts prepared by Joe Healy and his family, seen here. Healy, an educated Blood Indian, included a flaming plum pudding in his bill of fare.

kinds, and numerous cakes, awaited them, and everybody sat down to do full justice to the feast. A little bag filled with apples, candy and peanuts was handed to each child at the conclusion of this feast. The women were also given parcels of food for those of their families who were unable to attend.

Now let me relate an amusing incident that occurred to Mr. Healy in his endeavor to make a very happy Christmas for his children. At that time Mr. Healy had three children who had not yet been enrolled at the residential school and were still home with him. These were Johnny, Mary and Janie. Christmas Eve arrived. Mrs. Healy cautioned her offspring to behave and go to sleep early because Old Man — the Indian name for Santa Claus — was coming that night to give each one of them a present. But these children, curious to see Santa Claus, and a little fearful of what he might do to them if they were asleep when he arrived, stayed awake. Johnny occupied the edge of their bed, taking his position as protector of his two younger sisters who occupied the space nearest the wall.

Along towards morning Santa Claus came in cautiously with a bag on his back. Johnny, ever on the alert, espied him first, and thinking him to be a ghost of some description, or someone coming to do

68

them harm, jumped out of bed and, seizing the broom, started to inflict a very telling barrage of blows on Santa Claus. This unexpected reception caused him to retire in quick order, yelling as he did so, "Son, you are hurting me!" Thus did Santa Claus let the cat out of the bag!

Great excitement prevailed at the schools as the "Big Holy Day" approached. I remember distinctly my first contact with Santa Claus during my first year at school. I was only five at the time. We children had paraded to our school room where a large Christmas tree stood laden with gifts for all. After a short wait there was a great commotion near the entrance. Jingle bells could be heard outside and some of the staff laughingly ran towards the door to ascertain the cause of the uproar. An old man with a huge stomach and a white beard then made his appearance. Some of us children began to scream loudly and crawl under every available school desk. Others got behind some of the teachers, holding on to their legs for dear life. One boy named Arthur White Buffalo did the ostrich stint by sticking his head into a big cast-iron heater. It was some time before out teachers could calm us and not before we saw Santa Claus drop down on the floor, scattering a huge bag of candy, apples and peanuts in all directions, which caused his stomach to diminish in size. After this we enjoyed Santa Claus's visit, especially when he began to distribute the numerous gifts from the Christmas tree.

After that first year I always looked forward with great joy to Christmas Day. As time passed the Spirit of Goodwill spread among us Indians generally. Different lodges undertook the task of playing host to others at big dances and feasts. Unlike the white people, who solicit public donations for any charitable enterprise, the Indian societies require their members to contribute towards any undertaking sponsored in their name.

I remember one Christmas "at home" sponsored by the secret Horn Society. Each of its officers donated ten dollars and five dollars was contributed by the rank and file. The sum thus collected enabled this society to entertain at a great feast and dance not only local Indians but also visiting tribesmen from other reserves. At these Christmas dances visiting Indians were given a place of honor at the back of the hall facing the entrance. A visiting Indian was not required to dance unless asked to do so by a local woman, who gives him a present for this privilege. In all Indian dances the ladies ask the men to dance with them.

Now let us imagine ourselves participating at a Christmas dance and feast on the Blood Reserve. A large hall, built with round walls, serves as a community hall. Here all Christmas dances are held. The society officiating as host at a Christmas dance and feast assigns various duties to its members. One will be required to haul firewood and water to the community hall. Others will be detailed to clean out and decorate. One member will be asked to arrange for lights and coal oil, and a young man will be detailed to chop up all wood available for heating purposes.

People start arriving at the hall at about dusk. Wagon loads of Indians coming over the hills will be seen at intervals. A young man riding his pony will be seen approaching the hall, singing at the top of his voice. Hundreds of Indians in festive mood congregate to celebrate this greatest of all Christian festivals. Strange faces will be noticed among those present. These are visitors from neighboring reserves. They are quickly led forward by one of the committee and given seats on the floor in the space reserved for visitors. Seating arrangements are cared for by placing all women on one side and men on the opposite. A platform in the centre is reserved for drummers and singers. Boxes of groceries are also piled high in the centre.

Dancing begins to the beating of drums and singing. This is kept up at intermittent intervals, the braves dancing by themselves first, followed by the ladies asking the men to dance with them. Lunch is served at midnight, three or four chieftains playing hosts on this occasion, and a corresponding number of table cloths spread out on the floor. The guests sit around these table cloths. A progressive Indian playing host would have his wife bake cakes, pies and loaf bread for this special occasion. A less progressive host would have boiled meat and fried bread on his table cloth.

I remember a Christmas party which I attended on the Peigan Reserve. One of the hosts at a table cloth spread on the floor was an old Indian named Big Face Chief. I had noticed the old fellow after he started to spread his cloth. First he got hold of a huge pan of buns which he scattered broadcast all over the cloth. Then someone called to him from the opposite side of the hall. He immediately kicked the buns aside with his toes and walked across the table cloth. Later, I heard my name called as a guest at this particular table cloth. My excuse of having "just had supper" was ignored by a huge brave who led me forward by my right arm to the array of buns, and I sat down with a number of other Indians. I managed to slip a few of the buns in my pocket when no one was looking, which I later distributed to a gathering of boys loitering outside.

At these Christmas parties and dances the boxes of groceries piled high in the centre of the hall were given out as presents to aged people and visitors. Many hundred pounds of sugar were given out; jams of all descriptions, meat and bread were also issued. Candies, apples, and peanuts were not forgotten. Presents also were given to visiting Indians. These were in the form of money, bedding and clothing. The dance concluded about daylight, when all retired to their respective homes, sleepy and tired after the night's festivities.

Different schools on the reserve also celebrated an Indian day for Christmas. These took the form of huge feasts consisting of plum pudding and various other good things. An Indian school was a beehive of activity on such a day. Long hours of labor by the school staff were required to make a success of this undertaking. There is a saying that "an Indian treats his stomach as his god." Well, we sure did full justice to the hospitality of the school staff on such days and looked forward to the next time when we should again be invited. Hundreds of Indians from all parts of the reserve gathered on these occasions and everyone was treated to a good dinner. After everyone had adjourned to the school house, Santa Claus visited this huge gathering of tribesmen, where he distributed presents such as useful bits of clothing, overcoats, scarves and mitts.

As the season of Christmas drew near, towns and cities were visited by Indians in up-to-date cars, for the purpose of doing their Christmas shopping. Numerous toys were sold to the visiting tribesmen and many a little Indian child's wish was granted by good Santa Claus on Christmas morning.

Family parties were the order of the day at Christmas time, when Indians had the privilege of having with them their children, who were attending residential schools. Huge roasted turkey, with all the trimmings, was the chief item on an Indian Christmas menu. Highclass concerts were given by the pupils of the various Indian schools. The entertainments these Indian children participated in would do credit to them if staged in any big city.

To celebrate Christmas, Stoney Indians congregated at the village of Morley, west of Calgary. The bands from the north formed one line and those from the south another, and as they passed, each shook hands and wished the other a happy Christmas. This view was photographed in 1907.

"My Dear Child"

After Christmas in 1905, Anglican missionary John Tims wrote to his daughter, who was attending school in eastern Canada. In doggerel, he described their day at the Sarcee mission, west of Calgary, and their trip to have dinner with Rev. George Hogbin at the Calgary Indian Industrial School.

My Dear Child,
Would you like to hear the story
  How we spent last Xmas Day?
I would not think to tell you
  But you are so far away.

We'd service in the morning
  In the church that's up the lane.
It was filled to overflowing and
  With Indians in the main.

There were Crow Child and Jim Big Plume
  With their wives and children too,
Eagle Rib and Old Grasshopper,
  In all a motley crew.

They all stood at the entrance
  Of the church you know so well,
Mother, Miss McNutt & Sydney
  (Whose leg is not quite well.)

The parson in his surplice
  With his scarf & hood complete,
Also stood close to the entrance
  Of the church just up the street.

Wm. Stocken with a Kodak said
  All ready! there, that's good,
And he snapped the little shutter
  And photographed us as we stood.

Then we all went into service
  And we sang the Christmas Hymns
And we thanked God for the Saviour
  Who was born in Bethlehem.

The Fur Trade Frontier

Mother made for us the Music
  Using both her hands and feet,
And we all joined in the singing
  "Peace on Earth", as it was meet.

When we got back to the Mission
  We all prepared for lunch
Cold turkey & plum pudding
  And all good things at this lunch.

We next put in the horses,
  The sleigh that holds just 4
And when all were neatly seated
  We drove off from the door.

We started for the Hogbins
  Through the snow, some places deep.
We got on very nicely, till
  We reached the hill that's steep.

Then we had a small diversion
  For a bolt dropped from the sleigh,
Unless we had then seen it
  I'd p'raps not be writing you this day.

Uncle Jim & Reg looked for it
  Till their legs began to tire
Then we had to do without it
  And tie up the sleigh with wire.

We got safely to the Hogbins
  And the night was very fine,
We found them waiting for us
  For 'twas just time to dine.

We were just a merry party
  But we wanted one face more.
Can you guess whom I allude to?
  Well, the glass will tell you, sure.

There were just 14 for dinner
  The staff came in from the school
We had all the usual good things
And the "kids" ate to the full.

Then we placed chairs down the middle
  Of the room & marched around
To the tune of Hogbin's music
  And some sat upon the ground.

The chairs were not sufficient
  To accommodate us all
And now I've told the reason
  Why some of us got a "fall."

Well now I've told you truly
  How we spent last Xmas Day
So I had better stop here and
  Write more another day.

This is the photo that Archdeacon
J. W. Tims mentions in his poem.
Rev. Tims is at the right.

COMPLIMENTS OF THE SEASON

To Our Friends & Patrons

J. WESTON

CHRISTMAS WELCOME.

Dec. 1879.

Part II
The Pioneer Years

The construction of the Canadian Pacific Railway in the early 1880s opened the way for a flood of immigration which reached its crest at the turn of the century. The policy formulated by Sir Wilfrid Laurier in 1896 brought in masses of settlers from eastern Europe, the Scandinavian countries, and the United States so that within a few years the open prairies were dotted with new homesteads. Life was difficult for many settlers, particularly those who had no farming experience, but the offer of 160 acres of free homestead land was too tempting to ignore. Soon, such amenities as schools, churches, and railway branch lines made it possible for the pioneers to enjoy their new existence. Throughout this period, Christmas was an important event, celebrated in the custom of the homeland or adapted to the Canadian frontier.

Christmas, 1880

This editorial appeared in the Winnipeg Daily Times on Christmas Day, 1880, just as the West was beginning to experience an influx of settlers.

ere in the North-West, whose fertile leagues roll up even to the foot of the distant mountains that look down upon the western sea, will this Christmas — the first to many in the new land — be greeted with pathos, where sadness sifts in with hope? The look back to the dear old homes of rest so far away; the cherished and familiar firesides begirt for generations by forms twined in with fond remembrance, the household rites pertaining to the time; the holly and the mistletoe; the gathering of friends beneath the festal roof; the warmth, where kindred and neighbor ties found glad assurance. Hope should replume and gird herself anew, standing before memory clad in thoughts like these.

Yet as the land is goodly, so the men are strong. The sunshine of the day must wrap them in, however scattered, and to them, the stout forerunners of a future strength, goes out many a kindly thought upon this day when kindly thoughts abound. Here in our undoubted city, where the fated turkey trussed and ready for the spit is deaf alike to peal of bells or hum and hurry of the day; here where the destruction of all forms of toys goes on with tireless ardor by the over-caked and candy-ridden bands of boys, that quail not before uncounted pie, and rally freshly until astounded nature refuses to be rallied more; here at the "Gateway of the Plains" is food for all of fellowship high carnival, that would fain make tame the quaint and ruddy wish of old — to which we turn, extending to all — both far and near — a cordial Merry Christmas.

A Homestead Christmas

In recalling the events of her life, western Canadian author and supporter of women's rights, Nellie L. McClung, told of her first Christmas on her parents' homestead, five miles from Millford, Manitoba, in 1884.

Christmas was a jolly time that year. We had spruce boughs, brought from the Sandhills, across the doors and windows, and streamers of red tissue paper and red and green balls, made from tissue cut in circles, folded and sewed together. Mrs. Lundy had showed Hannah how to make these, when Hannah had stayed with her in the summer holidays. Mr. and Mrs. Lundy had a store about a mile east of Millford.

I remember particularly the apple-jelly tarts that we had at Christmas and how delicious they were. The apple-jelly was bright red in color, for snow apples were now sold in Mr. Lundy's store and mother had used only the parings and cores for the jelly, and the other part was made into apple sauce. Mr. and Mrs. Frank Burnett, Nina and Frankie, were our guests that year. A long table was set and no one had to wait for the second table.

Christmas Day has always been flavored to me with the pound cake and apple-jelly tarts of those first days in Manitoba.

A sod house in winter was a desolate scene on the western prairies. This view, published by *Harper's Weekly* in 1885, was part of a series on western Canada by Charles Graham.

The front-room always got a new coat of white-wash on the log walls at Christmas, and everything was scoured as white as sand or soap could make it. The hand-knit lace curtains, brought from Ontario, were washed and starched and stretched on home-made frames, so they would hang straight and reach the floor. Short curtains were considered slightly indecent. The two long widths of

rag carpet in bright stripes with orange warp were brought out and laid on the white floor, with the good mats, one hooked and one braided. The home-made lounge had a covering of dark maroon canton flannel and was well supplied with patch work cushions, crazy pattern of silks and satins and two log cabins, one made of "stuff pieces," the other one prints. There were two book-cases made with spools, painted black, and set with shelves and a "what-not" of five shelves, on which stood china ornaments, a shell box, with a green plush pin-cushion on the top, apples filled with cloves, and cups and saucers (honorably retired from active service because of cracks, or missing handles, but with these defects tactfully concealed in the way they were placed), colored glass mugs, and on the top, a bouquet of prairie grasses, set in a frosted glass vase, a lace pattern on deep blue. I remember it well, for I broke it years later, when bouncing a ball on the floor. Who would have thought a yarn ball would bounce so high?

When the weather got cold, the kitchen stove had to be brought into the big room, and it was a family grief when this change had to be made. If the weather did not come down too hard, the stove was kept out until after Christmas. Later when the storm doors and windows were added, and a bigger heater bought, a fine big barrel of a stove with a row of mica windows around its middle through which the coals glowed with all the colors of a sunset, the kitchen stove remained in the kitchen all winter.

But even when the kitchen stove was in the middle of the big room, there was a cheerful roominess about it. The woodbox papered with pictures of the Ice Palace, in Montreal, when covered with two boards over which a quilt was spread, made a nice warm seat and when we got the hanging lamp from Brandon, with a pale pink shade, on which a brown deer poised for a leap across a chasm, through which a green stream dashed in foam on the rocks, the effect was magical and in the pink light the white-washed walls were softened into alabaster.

We had two new pictures now, enlarged photographs of father and mother in heavy oak frames with a gilt edge, done by a travelling artist, who drove a team of mules and carried a few lines of tinware. Every family in the neighborhood had taken advantage of his easy plan to secure a lasting work of art. You paid only for the frame and received the picture entirely free though this offer might be withdrawn any minute for he was doing this merely to get his work known. He said there was no nicer way to give one's parents a pleasant surprise, and the pictures would be delivered in time for Christmas. When they came, we all had a surprise. We had thought that the seven dollars and thirty-five cents paid for both frames but we were wrong. Each one cost that amount and even at that the artist was losing money. The pictures were accepted and hung on the log walls, and in the declivities behind them were kept tissue paper patterns, newspaper clippings, and other semi-precious documents, thus relieving the congestion in the real archives, lodged in the lower regions of the clock, where notes, grain-tickets, tax receipts were kept.

Advertisement in the *Grain Growers' Guide,* December 6, 1916.

Facing page: Charles Wigg and his hired man posed for this Christmas picture at Lewisville, Alberta, about 1905.

79

Dear Grandma

In 1887, when she was fourteen years old, Maryanne Caswell emigrated with her parents from Ontario to an isolated homestead at Clark's Crossing, not far from the new town of Saskatoon. At Christmas, Maryanne wrote to her grandmother back in Ontario.

ear Grandma,

We made some Christmas cards to send to our relatives and friends in Ontario. We peeled and dried some birch bark off some of the wood pieces from the river bank. We selected our best pressed and dried flowers, that had retained their coloring, pasting them with egg white in a pleasing arrangement or design, sometimes stitching them. The spring flowers and autumn made the best showing but we are anxious to display the variety that grow on the wild prairies, so each family got different flowers and colorings. It was a problem to get white paper to wrap the finished cards for mailing so we wrapped them in yellow-brown building paper for security, and note paper for addressing. We were complimented on the results, so we are making some for our walls.

For Christmas gifts we had not any (like Simple Simon) but we exchanged some of our treasures and put them on a bare poplar tree, decorated some Chautauqua books Uncle Alex or A.K. had sent us with his usual Christmas letter. "May the Lord bless you and keep you and make his face to shine upon you and do you good."

For dinner we had a cherished wild goose stuffed with potato dressing seasoned with wild sage, vegetables, of course, suet pudding of grated carrots, flour and dried saskatoon berries boiled in a cloth.

Mother allowed us some hoarded sugar for taffy, flavoured with wild mint. Some of our pop-corn popped but not much pop in it. We danced on the threshing floor and in the evening played hide-and-seek and did some story reading by lamp for a treat as coal-oil is five dollars a gallon at Saskatoon.

At midnight Christmas Eve we girls went to the stable to see if the oxen would kneel as father said they would or did on Christmas Eve. We had never had the opportunity until now. When mother followed us out to the stable the oxen knelt for a second, as they got up they were disturbed. See?

We missed you and our old friends, Grandma. Everyone sends love.

Maryanne.

Roast Goose

This recipe appeared in The Emigrant, *a paper published in Winnipeg, in 1887.*

After it is picked, the plugs of the feathers pulled out and the hairs carefully singed, let it be washed and dried and a stuffing made of onions, sage, pepper, salt and bread crumbs (many like a few potatoes also in the stuffing); have a brisk fire, keep it well basted and roast according to size — a large goose, one hour and three-quarters, a moderate-sized one, one and quarter to one and a half hours. Serve with good gravy and apple sauce.

Facing page: This 1897 engraving shows Santa Claus with food, gifts, and a diary for the coming year.

81

The Cowboy's Christmas

The following poem was written on Christmas Day, 1893, by a High River, Alberta cowboy and later published in the Calgary Tribune.

Here in this land of the Wild West
   Away from sweethearts and lovers,
Distant from the scenes of our childhood,
   Away from our old-fashioned mothers,
Removed from the storm beaten cottage
   Where the ivy still tenderly clings;
Our absence makes a broken circle,
   Whilst we are like birds, on the wing.

Here in this land of the sunset,
   Years have gone since we said adieu;
Yet Christmas recalls to our memories
   The old faces and friends still true.
And tonight there's a depth of feeling,
   Which unbidden thrills each breast,
Whilst we sing of the now broken circle,
   Gathered in the old home nest.

They speak of our wild life on the plains;
   How we laugh while storms are high,
While sharing our lot with the kine,
   With our watchword to do or die,
They call us the wild daring cowboys,
   Forgetting that 'neath the rough vest
The heart may beat tender as woman's,
   Although with her charms unblessed.

Away then with dull care and sorrow;
   The years are hastening away,
Why should we think of the morrow,
   Why not drink and be merry today.
Then here's health to our dear old folks,
   To the friends still loving and true;
Here's health to the land of our fathers,
   And, Wild West, here's health to you.

In 1893, Calgary photographer
Robert Randolph Bruce brought
together this composite set of
views to produce his Christmas
card.

Letter to the Lonely

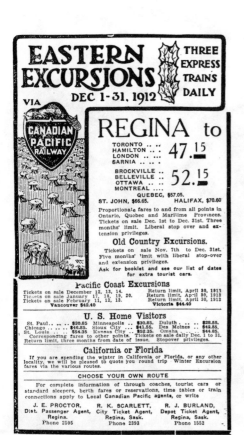
The author, Belle MacDonald, wrote a regular column for the Farm and Ranch Review under the title "Hearth and Home." She presented this open letter to her readers in 1906.

ow many different emotions are stirred by the approach of the Christmas season? Some can scarcely realize that it is Christmas again, so swiftly do the years fly when one is happy and busy. Others feel that they have lived an eternity since last Christmas Eve, so much has happened in the time, so many changes have come into their lives. Truly life is measured in heart throbbings and not in figures on a dial.

What changes has the past year brought in your life? Many are doubtless facing for the first time all the hardships of pioneer life. You almost dread Christmas; it will be so different from any Christmas. You will miss more than ever the dear friends you have left, and you will think of them all together — you alone missing.

Others are dreading Christmas time because a lonely grave on the prairie holds all that is left of one who was the light and joy of your home just a year ago. Your Christmas vision is a vacant chair, a desolated home and a grave. May the Kind Healer of all human sorrow help you to be strong, for your burden is heavy.

"Peace on earth and good will to men." That is our Christmas motto, which can be lived just as nobly in a shanty on the lonely prairie as it can in the largest city in the world. There are many lonely hearts and some bitter ones; cannot you bring peace to them?

Make special preparation for the Christmas season. You may not be able to spend any extra money. Well, never mind. Give the house an extra cleaning, and cook something extra, or if you cannot do that, dress a little better yourself. Make taffy for the children; only be sure to do something to mark the day and make it different from all the rest. You may try to forget, but you cannot. There is something about the ages old custom of Christmas that you cannot get away from.

Do not spend Christmas alone. There is always someone who would be very glad to celebrate Christmas with you. On the one day do not think only of your own pleasure, but think of the one who needs remembrance. "Peace on earth," that is your motto, and also "good will to men." Open your home to the one who needs you, and you will be living the Christmas teaching.

BACK HOME FOR CHRISTMAS!

Back home for Christmas! There's a whole library of thought in those simple words. They mean more than if you had been offered a five thousand dollar car, or a free ticket round the world, or a chance at being King or Queen of England.

Oh yes, of course, we know Christmas isn't like it used to be. (It never was, apparently). Not the same spirit—too much jazz----not a kid any longer---et cetera, et cetera. Too darned busy, no money, and all that. To all of which we might advise you to read that most celebrated and moving book entitled "The Christmas Carol" by Charles Dickens.

Some rather narrow-minded people think that there's a little too much overeating in Dickens and so on. H'm. Times have changed But the only thing Dickens hated was the solitary man. He hated him all the time, but most of all the kind of man who couldn't mix sociably and helpfully with his fellow creatures at this one season of the year that is a festival of human fellowship. Dickens wouldn't have had much use for the man who laughs at the idea of going back home for Christmas.

"Back Home" may mean a long way for you----but why not make a regular holiday of it this year? Shoot'em a wire back home that you're coming and are going to stay a week or may be more, and take Mother and the whole tribe along. How long ago is it, now, since you saw the old folks, and have they seen the young folks? And if it so happens that we're talking to the wrong party, and that YOURS is the "back home" that you want them to come to----why, we're not

talking to the wrong party at all! Send them a letter or a night-lettergram—now—that you're expecting them.

One word more. The best Christmas route, coming or going, to any part of Canada is

CANADIAN PACIFIC

a fast, frequent and comfortable train service with the highest standards of service in the world. See your station-agent right away about it.

A railway ad writer turned to some bad humor and purple prose to convince people that they should go home for Christmas.

Christmas Day For Lonely People

A few years after Mr. and Mrs. Harry Strange came from England to settle on a farm near Stettler, Alberta, Kathleen Strange began writing about farm life. Soon, her articles and essays were appearing in newspapers and magazines all across Canada, as well as in the United States and Britain. The following article was written for the Christmas edition of the Lethbridge Herald in 1929.

Since time immemorial the most approved method of extending goodwill and good cheer and of celebrating the festival of Christmas has been to invite one's friends and relatives to Christmas dinner.

In the 10 years that we have lived on the farm we have endeavored faithfully to live up to this old-time custom and in addition have endeavored to invite one or more people who would otherwise be forced to spend a lonely day. Our farm living room is large, the farm dining table capable of special extension, and we have one of the most welcoming features of all, a big open fireplace built from rocks found on our own land and in which burn huge logs from the hills around all winter long.

This custom of inviting lonely strangers to share our Christmas dinner is the result of one Christmas day that might have been very lonely and sad for us, the Christmas immediately following the Armistice, when my husband returned unexpectedly from France to find that all his own relatives as well as mine were out of London.

To our delight and surprise on Christmas morning at our hotel there arrived an invitation from their Majesties, the King and Queen, inviting us to a reception, concert and dance to be held at the Royal Albert Hall. It was being given by the King and Queen for all those officers, their wives and sweethearts, whose homes were abroad and who had not come to England with organized units but who had proceeded voluntarily to join up in the British forces.

Practically all the Royal family were present, including the King and Queen, Princess Mary, the Royal Princess, the Dowager Queen Alexandra and others, all of them entering in a wholehearted manner into the fun and happiness of the occasion and striving at all times to see that their guests had an enjoyable and memorable day.

The entertainment ended with an informal and very enjoyable dance, in which everyone, including members of the Royal family, indulged. Several of the younger members of the Royal family made it a special point to dance with as many of their guests as possible.

So happy were we that night when it was all over, and so great was the contrast between the day we had enjoyed and the dull and lonely day we had anticipated, that we there and then made up our minds that each forthcoming Christmas day we would make our own small effort to do something similar for any British people whom we might discover to be lonely and far from home.

This we have faithfully endeavored to do and have entertained for 10 Christmas days past, a succession of interesting, delightful and amusing strangers.

Christmas with Variations

I recall, for instance, one young bachelor from the elevator in a nearby town who turned out to be a Cambridge fellow who had taken the very highest of mathematical honors. Another out-of-work young man we picked just before Christmas on the streets of town, lonely and altogether disheartened, turned out to be member of one of England's oldest families. He was also a university graduate, out in Canada in an endeavor to make good. He told us he was always losing his jobs because he could not resist stopping whatever job he was doing to compose poetry when the inspiration seized him! Another man, who was regarded by many people as a grouch and a

The *Grain Growers' Guide* believed strongly in the institution of marriage if settlers were to survive the difficult years on the prairies. This 1909 illustration contrasts the bachelor or spinster with the married couple at Christmas. With six young children at her heels, one might question the tranquility of the married woman's life, but certainly not the spirit of her Christmas.

Construction men, all young bachelors, sat down to a special Christmas dinner in their railway boarding car during construction of the CPR bridge across the Saint Mary's River near Lethbridge in 1904.

very silent and unapproachable individual, was transformed by two glasses of port, into a most delightful dinner table companion and an intimate of the very best literature. Another guest we had to keep for several days and send for a doctor on account of his falling violently sick. It turned out to be a case of simple indigestion, but we later discovered that it was the first square meal the poor lad had eaten in several weeks. One of the very earliest of these lonely strangers we entertained has since attained no small success in farming. His appreciation of our slight hospitality for many years passed, has taken the form of presenting the farm every Christmas with an assortment of English delicacies that contributes to a real English Christmas dinner.

When the lights are turned low and the logs blaze warmly, and we are all sitting round the fireplace, many are the enjoyable and happy stories that pass back and forth, of adventures in curious parts of the world, and it is usually the stranger guests who contribute most to the success of the occasion.

Our thought has been to give a little happiness to others, but on looking back over the Christmas days that have passed, we are at one in thinking that we ourselves have probably had most of the pleasure. We have met some delightful and interesting people and have made many friends who have lasted through the years.

The Bachelor Homesteader

John Wilson had been a newspaperman in England before emigrating to Canada in 1905. After drifting through the Manitoba region for two years, he took a homestead south of Prince Albert, Saskatchewan, where he celebrated the Christmases he describes in this article. At that time, there were twice as many single men as women in Saskatchewan. This sometimes resulted in loneliness at Christmas, but not for the author.

spent my first Christmas on the prairie in 1907, shortly after I had commenced homesteading [about 35 miles from Duck Lake, Sask.] At that time I was full enough of enthusiasm to enjoy anything that had a spice of novelty about it. Christmas day I spent at the home of my friend Shepley with three other bachelor guests. It was different from any Christmas I had ever spent before, but not the least enjoyable by any means. We had very little of the usual paraphernalia of Christmastime. There was no Christmas tree, no holly, no mistletoe, and no girls to kiss under it if there had been.

But what really counts at Christmas is a spirit of good will, a good dinner and a good appetite to enjoy it. We had all of these. Shepley had been to town and might have stayed there over the festive season, but he would not disappoint the rest of us, and came back the night before with a pair of nice fat ducks and a plum pudding.

Railways surveyors for the Grand Trunk Pacific celebrated Christmas in 1908 by playing cards in their bunk house.

Christmas in the West

We all contributed something to the bill of fare, and took turns at cooking and sawing wood outside so that all should have appetites appropriate to the occasion. Chicken soup preceeded the roast duck, and plum pudding and mince pies followed, and the feeling of sweet content that seemed to steal over us all when we drew around the stove after dinner, made us forget the homesickness which we all no doubt felt, but which no one spoke about.

The second Christmas was different. We had by this time extended our acquaintance considerably, and had discovered that there were some ladies living in the neighborhood after all. We started to celebrate on Christmas Eve, and with two teams and sleighs gathered up a merry party of nearly twenty. We first went to a Doukhobor village, and with one of the ladies of the party dressed as Santa Claus, beard and all, visited each house leaving toys for the children and having a great time generally. Then we went off to

Christmas was a time for visiting by ranchers and farmers. Hitching up their sleighs or buggies, they traveled to neighboring farms to celebrate the holiday season. Above are teams lined up at the Millar ranch, south-west of Calgary, at the turn of the century.

another village, where the Catholic members of the party attended service before we returned home in the early hours of the morning.

The festivities were renewed as soon as we had had a few hours' sleep and had done our chores, and the whole neighborhood started on a round of visits which lasted till the New Year. Sometimes a bunch of a dozen or more of us would descend unannounced upon some unsuspecting bachelor just as he was preparing for bed and proceed to make ourselves at home in his shack. In case his pantry should not be well supplied, we always took some eatables along, as well as a few packs of cards and usually some kind of musical instrument.

When travelling on the prairie at night one is apt to get lost, so being careful people we generally waited for daylight and breakfast before dispersing. Those were good times, and no one who has not taken part in the social life of a prairie settlement can understand how enjoyable it can be made.

90

A Parson's Diary

When thousands of immigrants came to the prairies at the turn of the century, they sent up a cry for clergymen to serve their new districts. Britons responded with a campaign called the Archbishop's Western Canada Fund, which raised money to send young Anglican ministers from the old country. One of these men, the Rev. C. Travers Melly, arrived at Imperial, Saskatchewan late in 1914 and recorded his pioneering activities during that Christmas season.

ednesday, December 23rd — After household duties I start off about 11:30 a.m. on my motor-cycle along a main road, partly good and clear, partly rough and icy, to Simpson, seven and a half miles. Dinner with a good friend and borrow his horse. Ride across country another seven miles to a country schoolhouse to take part in a Christmas entertainment and to act Father Christmas. Start back about 5 p.m. to Simpson. Leave horse and start off again on motor-cycle. Arrive at 8 p.m., at which hour the Christmas tree entertainment starts. As I have to act in the cantata there, I have to change my clothes pretty quickly. Rush across and arrive just five minutes before my call. Affair went off well. Get supper and have a chat with some friends. By the way, on the Christmas tree was a silk scarf and pair of hair brushes from my congregation.

Christmas Day — Up and light the fire in the church. Tidy up self and house. Christmas Communion 9:30 a.m. — twenty present. Put on innumerable wraps while one of the ladies gets me a small breakfast. Off on bike to Simpson, seven and a half miles. Arrive 11:30 a.m. Warden has got the fire going and the Communion vessels ready. Christmas Communion. Dinner with some good friends of mine and play with their children. Then some music, supper, and card games. A quiet but most enjoyable Christmas. 10 p.m. begin to say I must go to bed, but we get talking on religion and it is 12:30 before I get off to my shack. Bed at 1:15 a.m.

Saturday, 26th — Innumerable odds and ends and a feeling of slackness and a wish that Sunday did not come so soon. Motor-bike back to Imperial. Get mail, letters, etc. Light fire, draw water out of my tank under the cellar floor and fetch my fruit out of the paper-padded box down there, which keeps it from frost when I am away. If I left them in the room the fruit would go rotten and the water freeze solid and burst the bucket or tank. Work out sermon between the visits of two men who are great friends.

Sunday, 27th — Up at 7:45 a.m. Telephone out to Rouse country district to ask if I am to come. It is a cold, windy morning, with probably between thirty and forty degrees of frost. I am ready to go if the people will turn out. Someone offers to light the fire in the schoolhouse there and have things ready. All right. I start at 9:20 a.m. after a light breakfast and motor-cycle along a main road for six miles. In a sleigh five and a half miles more over snow. No fire, no one there. Must feed the horses. I light a fire in the stove. It is frightfully cold in this cold room, at least ten degrees below zero. Suddenly up come two men and the wife of one of them, a communicant, who has never been able to get to Communion since I began to have Holy Communion there twelve months ago. Also she brought her baby to be baptized. So after it seemed that we should have no service at all, we have had a baptism, which would have been almost impossible to manage for the next three months, and our Christmas Communion with six present. The drive back is not so cold, the wind having dropped. Reach Lucas' farm at 2:40 p.m. Five minutes to swallow some lunch and start off down to Imperial for Evensong. About twenty-four present. Wrap up and set off again before it gets late. Arrive 6:30 p.m. at my neighbour's house at Simpson, where they have a lovely hot supper waiting. Hurry across to church to take Evensong there. Congregation of twenty-four. A group of us adjourn to the shack, where I have not had time to light the fire. Two wardens are in from the country for service, so we get some important cheques signed and business done. But my ink has frozen solid and the fountain pen ink freezes as it reaches the nib. I borrow ink from a neighbour and it too freezes as we write. So we have to dip the pen into the ink and hold the pen over the lamp and write quickly. Then to the house of a member of the congregation for coffee and cake and a glorious smoke.

Even the most roughly built pioneer church was decorated for Christmas. Above is Saint Clare's Roman Catholic church at Val Soucy, which served the Ukrainian settlers north of Redwater, Alberta.

Letters from the West

Monica Hopkins arrived in western Canada in September 1909, meeting her husband "Billie" who had gone ahead to establish a ranch near Priddis, southwest of Calgary. A few months later, she wrote to a friend in Australia, telling her about Christmas in the West. Joe and Harry were the hired men, while Helene was a childhood friend visiting from England.

earest Gill:
The happiest of New Years and all the best to both of you. We loved the parcel of books that arrived just the mail before Christmas. We didn't open them until Christmas morning; books are a real joy to get here and your selection was delightful, suited all our tastes. Joe retires into *Robbery Under Arms* every evening now, and there is never a peep out of him. It will take him weeks to read for he is a slow reader; fortunately Billie read it first or he would have been annoyed at having to wait so long. I haven't read it, just glanced through it, but I don't think it is much my style; I prefer the less "bluggy" ones. Thank you so much for them, you certainly need not have apologized for sending books in place of some things more useful. We would rather have books than anything, so send along as many as you like, and as often as you wish.

We had a very nice Christmas Day, though I was disappointed at getting no home parcels or letters. We had quite a lot of English parcels from friends but they were not quite the same; still they made our breakfast table look very festive. Joe had never seen parcels on a breakfast table before. I rather doubt if he has had many presents before and he was quite thrilled at those we gave him and very distressed that he had none for us, but he has not been to Calgary since he was in to meet us. Billie, the young spendthrift, had all sorts of things for me and made my pipe, slippers and book for him look very humble.

I had a tremendous spread, had been cooking for days and the old hens came up to scratch and I take back all the nasty things I said about them in my last letter! After a huge dinner we went skating on the creek. Joe, as most Canadians, is a really good skater. I can manage to keep going fairly but Billie is a perfect menace on skates; he wobbles in every direction, his arms going around like windmills.

He goes where his skates take him, clutches at all and sundry, and finally sits down with the most awful whack, is up again and on in another direction. I keep clear of him for a very little thing upends me. We had a jolly time and returned home ravenous to eat huge quantities of cold turkey, pudding, mince pies and trifle, and after washing up we sat down to eat fruit, nuts, and chocolates, and to read your good books. It was a happy thought on your part to send them. Thank you again.

On Boxing Day, Joe drove to Priddis and oh joy! returned with my missing parcels, and parcels for Billie from Ireland. Just as we had unpacked everything and the room was knee deep in paper, all the Mortons arrived. Such a mess, but I bundled the paper away and left them to look at our gifts while I got them a meal. As it was a cold day I gave them hot soup as a starter and then cold scraps of everything that was left over. They only stayed about three hours as they had a long drive and the nights are very cold. It's down below zero nearly every night now. My parcels from home were lovely. Mother and Father still think that we are more or less on the verge of starvation and that we can only get the absolute essentials out here in the way of wearing and household goods and I have no intention of disillusioning them at present.

Our love to you both,
Monica

A year later, in December of 1910, Mrs. Hopkins sent the following note to the same friend.

Dearest Gill:
I think I told you that Helene and I were going to have a few days in Calgary. We had a very nice time, though we were pretty well on the "go" all the time. We had so many presents to buy, not only for ourselves but we had been given several commissions by neighbours as well, and it's hard to do shopping for other people. The shops looked very festive and there were lovely things to buy, had we the money, which needless to say we had not. Still, we managed to get some quite nice things to send home. Last year Billie and I sent so many pairs of moccasins that one would almost think our people were centipedes! We felt we couldn't send any more this year so we got them gauntlet gloves made by the Stoneys, with lovely bead work and fringes. If they don't care to wear them they will make very nice souvenirs. It was fine but cold and a democrat is not the warmest of conveyances. One is so high up the wind seems to catch you from every corner of the globe.

While Helene and I were waiting at the store in Priddis for Billie to come for us, a motorcar drove up and two people got out, tourists we imagined them to be. Everything seemed to amuse them; they laughed at a saddle horse tied to a rail, at a wagon standing outside. They even laughed at the outside of the store, which certainly to my mind is nothing to laugh at, it's ugly enough to make the angels weep! Then they came into the store and evidently found the inside

94

and its occupants even funnier than the outside. That they were Yankees was evident, not young, around forty I would say. He was a nondescript sort of man, while his wife looked as if she had been dissolved and while liquid had been poured into her clothes and allowed to set — what they called in the States "A Stylish Stout."

They wanted some ci-gars and candy and they asked Mrs. Dennis how she ever sold anything in this "neck of the woods." Mrs. Dennis was splendid, instead of getting annoyed as I should have done, and giving them back as good as they gave, she answered them quietly and politely and when the female asked her "For the land's sake, what do you do here in the winter?" Mrs. Dennis told her there were dances, the young people skated and went visiting. Just as if life was one long social round. The lady sniffed unconvinced and said, "It may suit you but it would drive me off my nut. I guess you have to have been used to nothing else to be able to stand it." Then, eyeing Helene and me, who were standing quite close by and simply fuming at her rudeness, said to Helene, "I suppose you were born here?" Helene drew herself up and asked in an imperious voice, "Were you speaking to me? If you were, it may interest you to know that I come from Sydney, Australia, and that I love this life." The lady looked a little subdued and asked me if I was born here, to which I replied in my very best "Oxford voice" that I was English but hoped to make Priddis my home, and that I, too, loved the life. The couple prepared to leave, the lady slightly deflated, but after all she got in the last word, for as she was going through the doorway she said in a loud voice, "I wonder you don't die of green mould!" and neither Helene nor I could think of anything worthwhile to say, so we remained silent.

Since our return we have not been out. We both caught wretched colds in our heads and have sniffed and sneezed in the most trying manner, and wallowed in camphor and eucalyptus, in hopes of loosening our colds and preventing others in getting them. So far the men have escaped and we are feeling better. We have made the puddings and cakes, also the mince meat. During the summer when eggs were plentiful, I packed several hundred in water glass so that now I am able to make my cakes without waiting for those miserable old hens to condescend to lay an egg. I am able to thumb my nose at the old wretches when I go in to feed them and find divil an egg in the nest boxes and so, out of pure cussedness, the old brutes have started to lay!

Our parcels from home arrived some time ago and are reposing in the bathroom and every day I go in and shake them and sniff. I hope I shall be able to hold out until Christmas Day before I open them. The declaration forms read most delightfully, all sorts of nice things to eat and wear! They were so distressed to hear last year that the parcels were late that evidently they made up their minds to be in good time this Christmas. Billie has a parcel from Ireland and Helene one from Australia — nothing from you yet — wretch — but there are nearly two weeks so I haven't given up hope yet.

I must leave this now, the dogs are barking and Helene has just said there are riders at the west gate.

Christmas in the West

Facing page: The Farmers Supply Company of Winnipeg offered a number of Christmas specials to its customers in 1916. However, a hand-pumped washing machine, at lower right, might not be some people's idea of a perfect Christmas gift.

Santa Claus was the theme of this 1929 puzzle for readers of the *Grain Growers' Guide*.

Three weeks since I started this letter and Christmas and New Year's are over, and we have all recovered from the extra "festive fare" and all the work that it makes. Harry provided the main part of the dinner. The turkey, which he won curling at Priddis, was a whopper, twenty-nine pounds and my very largest dish only just held him (the sausages had to be served separately); he was delicious and so tender. The pudding and mince pies were voted a great success. The Christmas cake iced with angelica and cherries really looked quite professional. I was very proud of it. Christmas Day was cold and blustery and we didn't go out at all, ate, slept, and ate again! In the evening we played cards. Our parcels took a long time to open, everyone at home had excelled themselves, and the mild hints that I have been sending all through the year had evidently fallen on good ground and multiplied themselves accordingly! Bless them!

> Good-bye and good night,
> and our love to you both.
> Monica

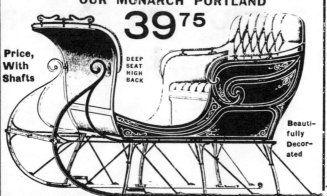

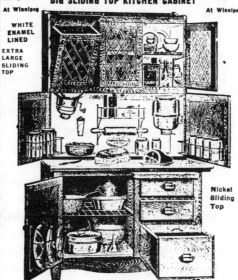

How to Prepare a Turkey

Helen Wainwright wrote a regular column, "With the Cook," in the Farm and Ranch Review, published in Calgary. The following advice to young housewives appeared just before Christmas in 1911.

he principal feature of a Christmas dinner is usually the turkey. I have seen young housewives as ignorant about the preparation of a fowl for the table as if she had never eaten one. Hence we will give in detail the different processes through which the Christmas turkey goes before he finds himself under the carver's knife.

To Kill a Turkey

There is a right and wrong way to kill a turkey. The proper way is to tie the turkey up by the feet to a nail in the wall. Hang a weight, a small flat iron will do, around the head of the fowl, and just before the weight is let down, pierce the artery in the neck with a small sharp knife. This allows the fowl to bleed without getting the blood over the feathers and body. When the turkey is dressed and cleaned immediately for family use this, of course, is not so particular.

To Dress a Turkey

Pluck the feathers. When the turkey is very young, the skin is often so tender that it is severely broken during the plucking process. This detracts from the appearance of the fowl, so it usually is better to scald the fowl in boiling water. Then the feathers can be easily plucked. The fowl must be merely dipped in the water and removed almost immediately.

The hair and down are removed by singeing. This is done by holding the turkey over a flame (burning paper does nicely), and constantly changing its position until all parts have been exposed to the flame. Cut off the head and pull out the pin feathers by means of a small pointed knife. Cut through the skin around the leg one and one-half inches below the leg joint, care being taken to not cut the tendons; place the leg at this cut over the edge of the table, press downward to snap the bone, then take foot in right hand, holding bird firmly in left hand and pull off the foot, and with it the tendons.

In old birds, the tendons must be drawn separately, which is best accomplished by using a steel skewer. This may not be very easy but

98

the tendons are very tough and sinewy and make the drumstick not so pleasant eating as when they are removed.

Next make an incision through the skin below the breast bone at one side of the vent. Cut around the vent and if care has been taken, the hand can be inserted and the whole contents, entrails, gizzard, heart and liver, can be withdrawn without breaking the sack which contains them. The gizzard, heart and liver constitute the giblets.

The gall bladder lies under the liver and great care must be taken that it be not broken, as a small quantity of the bile which it contains would impart a bitter taste to the parts with which it comes in contact.

Enclosed by the ribs on either side of the backbone may be found the lungs of soft consistency and red color. Every part of them must be removed. The kidneys lie in the hollows near the end of the backbone, and must also be removed. Place two fingers under the skin at the neck and pull out the windpipe. Also, the crop (which should be empty) will be found adhering to the skin close to the breast.

Drawn down the skin and cut off the neck close to the body, leaving the skin much longer to turn back under the body. Remove the oil bag on the top of the tail, and wash the fowl but do not allow it to soak in water. Wipe inside and out, looking carefully to see that everything has been withdrawn.

Separate the gall bladder from the liver, cutting off all parts that have a greenish tinge. Remove the arteries, veins, and clotted blood from the heart. Cut the fat and membranes from the gizzard. Make a gash through the thickest part of the gizzard and cut as far as the inner lining, being careful not to pierce it. Remove and discard the inner sack. Wash giblets and cook until tender with the neck and tips of wings, putting them in cold water and bringing water to a boil that some of the flavor may be drawn out into the stock which is to be used for making gravy.

SUCH A FINE DINNER.

Medicine Hat News,
December 20, 1894.

To Stuff a Turkey

Put stuffing by spoonfuls in neck end, using enough to make the bird look plump when served. Allowance must be made for the swelling of crackers, otherwise the skin may burst during the cooking. Stuff the body and sew up the skin.

To Truss a Turkey

Draw thighs close to body and hold by inserting a steel skewer under middle joint, running it through the body, coming out under middle joint on the other side. Fasten the legs together at the ends and tie securely with a long string to the tail. Place wings close to the body and hold them by inserting a second skewer through the wing, body and the wing on the other side. Draw the skin under the back and fasten with a small wood skewer.

This trussing makes a bird look plump and fat.

To Roast a Turkey

Place on its back on a rack in a dripping pan. Rub entire surface with salt, and spread breast and legs with three tablespoons of butter

Christmas dinner, 1908, at the
T. A. Kitts home in Manitoba.

mixed with two tablespoons of flour. Dredge the bottom of the pan with flour. Place in a hot oven, and when the flour is browned reduce the heat, and baste. Add two cups hot water. Baste every ten minutes until the fowl is done, which will be about three hours.

During the cooking, turn the turkey often that it may brown evenly. Before serving, remove strings and skewers. Garnish with parsley or celery tips. Do not neglect this last as it greatly increases the appearance of the bird and appearance goes a long way toward enticing the appetite.

Giblet Gravy

Pour off the liquid in the roasting pan. Return six tablespoons of fat to the pan and brown with six tablespoons of flour. Pour on very gradually three cups of liquor in which the giblets, etc., were cooked. Cook five minutes, season with salt and pepper; strain and add the finely chopped giblets.

Stuffing

Remove the crust from a loaf of stale bread, crumb it thoroughly, add powdered sage or poultry dressing, salt and pepper. Pour over a half a cup of boiling water in which one half cup of butter has been melted.

To Carve a Turkey

The bird should be placed on its back, with legs at right of platter for carving. Introduce carving fork across breastbone, hold firmly in left hand. With the carving knife, cut through skin between leg and body, close to body. With the knife pull back the leg and disjoint from the body. Then cut off the wings. Remove the leg and wing from the other side. Slice the meat from the breast in thin crosswise slices. Remove the fork and disjoint the legs and wings. Serve a slice of white meat with each piece of dark meat.

North-West of Sixteen

In his reminiscences, author James G. MacGregor tells of his boyhood days on the family homestead near Westlock, Alberta. In particular, he recalls a Christmas shortly before World War I. Obviously the MacGregor family had not read Mrs. Wainwright's advice on the proper way to kill and prepare a turkey!

ecember 24 dawned upon a light fall of fresh, fluffy snow. A good breakfast of fried moose liver and fried potatoes started us off to a proper enjoyment of the great day. No work, except the necessary chores, was done that day, although Joe and Dad opened the case of whisky [the year's Christmas cheer] and fortified themselves against possible frost-bite. Axel Clausen came over, and the three men communed together at one side of the big kitchen. Bill and I played about in the snow with Gyp, one of a long succession of dogs all named Gyp. As dusk began to gather, a dozen or so turkeys sought roosts on the roof of the henhouse, on the hay rack, and even in a tree or two. One of them, a huge gobbler, had been fattened with care. His flight to the top of the henhouse reminded Mother that it was time to kill him, so that he could hang till New Year's Day. Accordingly, she called upon the three men to go out and slay the gobbler, promising to have supper ready by the time they had done so. But one story led to another, and supper was ready before the deed was done.

"All right," said Mother, "right after supper, then."

After supper the men sallied forth to the woodpile for the axe, while Bill and I, hopping about in anticipation, ran ahead to point out the last roosting-place of the turkey gobbler on top of the henhouse.

But it was not just as simple as the men had planned. The gobbler, aroused by the hullabaloo, craned his long neck and tried to make out the reason for all this uproar. Five voices rose on the evening air, shouting at him to come down; for who could get at him there? A sixth voice awakened all the sleeping turkeys as Gyp joined in. The impressive bird gobbled in annoyance. From their posts high above the yard — from the hay rack, the trees, and the barn roof — lesser gobblers joined the medley, while turkey hens chattered nervously.

"Throw something at him," suggested Joe; and a rain of missiles

A popular rural activity at Christmas was a turkey shoot. Actually, no turkeys were shot; targets were used and the winners took home the prized birds. The above advertisement appeared in the *Calgary Tribune* in 1888.

101

clattered on the henhouse roof, all falling short but alarming the hens, so that they added their voices to the din. Chappie and Charlie, who had previously been dozing over at the straw-pile, were aroused and came galloping in to share the fun. Bunty, secure in the cow barn, raised her voice.

"Get your twenty-two and shoot him," suggested Axel.

"But I don't want to make holes in him," muttered Dad.

"Get a pole and wire, and snare him."

"Get a ladder and the pitchfork."

"Where's Jim's bow and arrow?"

The pole and the snare-wire seemed to be the best bet, but elbows that had bent all afternoon were not connected with steady hands and the wire only tickled the gobbler. Other turkeys left their perches and milled around the yard in alarm, but the prize of the flock refused to leave the safety of the henhouse.

"Let's go back to the kitchen and steady our nerves and talk things over while the turkeys settle down," said Joe. Since this was the most practical idea brought forward so far, it was adopted with only Bill and me and Gyp dissenting.

The consultation refreshed the men and they came out filled with new determination. This time they came brandishing Dad's salmon rod, complete with a hundred feet of fishing line and a lump of lead dangling at the end of it. They marched resolutely on the henhouse, but the gobbler had flown. He was soon located in the company of three disturbed turkey hens behind the straw-pile. As the chase was resumed, he registered annoyance and stamped on the ground. When three determined men rushed at him from three different directions, he neatly eluded them by flying to the top of the pile. Here he rocked with anger, pointing his out-thrust head down at his pursuers, while flaming away in the moonlight his red wattles swayed in time to his angry gobbling.

"Swish," went the salmon rod; "creak, creak," sang the reel; and "whack" went the lump of lead against his long wing feathers. The cast, intended to encircle his neck or legs, had missed. The challenging gobbler stopped abruptly as anger gave way to anxiety, and he flew down the other side of the pile and ran off.

The tempo of pursuit quickened as the gobbler, leading a dozen or so frightened hens, streaked around the barn and raced off through the trees. Axel led the attackers, with Joe right behind, while Dad, having difficulty getting the fishing rod through the trees, trailed slightly. And behind him came Gyp, two boys, and Chappie and Charlie. The gobbler flew to the top of the chicken-house, but Axel clattered so much when he tripped over the neck-yoke of the sleigh that the bird unwisely left this security and the mad rout started all over again. He flew to the top of the hay rack, and loomed against the bright sky like a vulture as he peered about anxiously.

"Try sneaking up on him," said Joe; "we'll wait here and you slip around into the shadow of the biffy. From there a good cast should get him," So, while we all watched tensely, Dad sneaked up on the vigilant gobbler. This time the lump of lead whirled around the gobbler's outstretched neck and we had him. The chase which had occupied a thrilling hour was over. Tranquillity settled over the yard. The moon cast stark shadows on the trampled snow. The rabbits ventured back to the woodpile. Reluctantly Bill and I heeded the summons to bed.

In the excitement we had forgotten that it was Christmas Eve. "Hurry up and go to sleep," said Mother, "for Santa Claus will be along any minute now; and you know what happens if he comes around and little boys are not asleep — he goes away again."

Go to sleep on Christmas Eve? When ideas of Christmas and of Santa raced after each other through a boy's head? Why, you might as well take him to a circus and tell him to go to sleep. If, for an hour, he has galloped about in the moonlight in all the excitement of capturing the turkey gobbler, that makes it all the more impossible. For what seemed like hours, Bill and I turned and tossed, afraid of offending Santa Claus and trying desperately to go to sleep.

Downstairs, as Mother worked in the kitchen, pots and pans

As children dream of Christmas, their mother brings out her few treasures for their stockings. This nostalgic scene appeared in the *Calgary News-Telegram* in 1913.

rattled. Snatches of talk drifted up to us as Dad, Axel, and Joe reviewed parts of the recent chase. I became anxious, then angry, and marching to the head of the stairs I scolded all and sundry for keeping us awake, and for scaring Santa away. Mother came up to soothe our taut nerves, and just then from far down the road came the tinkling of Santa's sleigh-bells. Even Mother stood in the darkness and listened as the sound of the bells came nearer. Up the road they came; twice around the house they swung — then paused. Right out there in the moonlit yard, just beyond the blind which we dared not pull aside, Santa and his reindeer waited and listened, trying to find out if all in the house were sound asleep. We dared not look out, because at the least peek he would discover us and away he would go. But you can't fool Santa. In a moment, with a gentle tinkle, his reindeer started up, and we could hear the receding bells as they made off rapidly past the barn and over the fields towards Paulson's.

It was life's bitterest moment. Santa had come, heard the three men talking downstairs, and at the sound had passed us by. He would not return till next Christmas, if then. We had been tested and found wanting. If we were not asleep, it was not our fault; the blame lay on everybody else, on poor Mother, and especially on Dad, Axel, and Joe. Anger rose above our anguish. All the adults came in for bitter denunciation. That over, Bill and I lay down to sleep. The excitement of the hunt and the anticipation of Christmas had given way to despair.

What wakes boys so early on Christmas morning? When the first streaks of dawn breasted Tracy's hill, swept down over the east field and lighted the roof of the barn, Bill and I were awake, peering into the gloomy recesses of the room. There, at the foot of the bed, were two stockings fairly bulging with oranges, nuts, and toys. On either side of the bed were packages, a drum, a mechanical clown, books, and mittens, and moccasins. Santa Claus had relented, and the world was whole again. How were we to know that Santa had been very late making his rounds that night and that what we had heard was only Joe Fowlie running around ringing a set of sleigh-bells?

Christmas morning on the farm! You can't describe it. It's just a jumble of fleeting, gleeful moments as a boy's happiness jumps from this joy to that. Breakfast? Who wants breakfast, with nuts and oranges, apples and candy piled all over the place? Who has time for breakfast with drums to beat, clowns to wind, and books to read? Even Tabby the cat know it's Christmas as with tail held straight aloft she stalks around, sniffing at teddy-bears, toying with wrapping-paper, or playing with a piece of string dangling from the large red Christmas bell in the centre of the room. Even Gyp, waiting outside, ever ready to welcome two boys emerging from the house, and keen to get into whatever deviltry seizes their attention — even Gyp knows it. And Bunty, as she turns her head to watch the milking, munching the while at an extra ration of oats, Bunty knows it's Christmas. Chappie and Charlie, chomping over extra bundles of greenfeed thrown down from the loft, know something is afoot as the barn door is opened to let them out to gallop and frisk

Facing page: Christmas at the Bow River Horse Ranch, west of Calgary, in 1904 was complete with tree and presents. Enjoying their gifts are the ranch owner's children, Victor and Everette Goddard.

104

and kick up their heels on the way to the water trough. Then, when you want to put them in the barn again to harness them, they pretend that they can't find the door. Inching slowly along, they stop to look in as if dimly they recognize it but are not quite sure. And then with a toss of the head and a flip of the tail, they swing off and gallop round and round the barn. But it's all part of the fun, for they too are going to Johnstone's for Christmas Day.

Going to Johnstone's! You can get in your airliners and fly to Hawaii for Christmas. You can motor to Los Angeles for Christmas and the Rose Bowl Game. You can assemble in Times Square and sway with the crowd as the New Year comes in. But for me — I would like to turn back the years and celebrate another Christmas Day at Johnstone's!

Let Dad hitch Chappie and Charlie to the sleigh. Let Mother bundle her boys up in coats and mitts and scarves. Let her fill the sleigh with straw, blankets, and cushions, and carry out two stones heated in the oven to keep their feet warm. Let her tuck everybody in. Let Dad, in his old sheepskin coat and moccasins and his moth-eaten old muskrat hat, flip the lines to the horses as they start. Let all hear the bob of the bunks, the swish of the runners over the packed snow, and the tinkle of the heel chains, as gaily we swing down the trail. For today we are going to Johnstone's for Christmas dinner.

Christmas dinner at Johnstone's! That was an experience never to be forgotten — an experience, alas, no longer possible to duplicate. Yet the recipe for it is simple. Take the hungry stomach of an active farm boy that gnaws again an hour after any meal. Give it a breakfast cut short by the excitement of new toys. Bundle stomach and boy into heavy clothes, and whisk them in a farm sleigh two miles through the crisp spruce-scented air. Let the boy run into Mrs. Johnstone's kitchen. Let the aroma of roasting turkey fill his nostrils and the crackling of the basting fat assail his ears. That is your recipe.

Garnish, if you wish, by letting his eyes dart about the kitchen. See there on the shelf are six pies, two blueberry, two mince, and two low-bush cranberry, still hot from the oven, their acrid smell blended with the odour of hot lard. On the stove, bubbling away in the big pot, is the Christmas pudding, its savoury steam competing in gusto with the other smells. Let this boy stand looking through the doorway with his back to the crackling kitchen and before him the long log room (usually part dining-room, part sitting-room, but today all dining-room). Let his eyes take in the red Christmas bell in the centre, with its green paper streamers sweeping off to the corners of the room, and then the long table set for ten, and loaded with colourful, cheery Christmas goodies. Look at the piles of home-made crusty bread, the plates of cookies, plain or iced with red or green, and the red candles flickering their welcome. Look at the green of the cucumber pickles, the yellow of the mustard pickles and the glowing red of pickled beets. And there, on the sideboard, right there enthroned in the very centre — that is Mrs. Johnstone's chocolate cake. What a cake! Made as only Mrs. Johnstone can

106

Friends and family at the C. A. Hamilton farm, nine miles from Baldur, Manitoba were dressed in their finest for this 1910 Christmas dinner.

make it. Five inches high — two layers, chinked with jam and roofed with a quarter inch of chocolate icing. And there to keep it company stands the huge bowl filled with preserved wild strawberries and flanked by two piles each of five ruby glass dessert dishes, while tucked into every vacant space on the sideboard are bowls of nuts, oranges, apples and candy, a plate of jelly-roll and a pile of cinnamon buns. Over all presides Mrs. Johnstone, beaming with friendship and with Christmas time and with pride in her handiwork.

Let this boy walk slowly around the table and see all the side dishes — here a dish of low-bush cranberry jelly waiting for the turkey, there a jar of high-bush cranberry jelly, and there some spiced black currants. Finally the glistening bowls awaiting the arrival of potatoes and carrots, and, beside each of the ten white plates, flanking each knife and fork, red, yellow, and green Christmas crackers.

Then, amidst all these smells and sights, make him wait nearly an hour while the turkey roasts to its brownest crackling excellence. Then seat everybody. Otis Johnstone at the head, his face beaming and his bald head shining, while he whets away at the huge carving-knife made from a piece of scythe blade and hafted with deer horn.

Then let Mrs. Johnstone carry in the turkey, while Mother brings bowls piled high with mashed potatoes, white and fluffy, and with rich golden carrots, and the steaming dark brown gravy. Have Otis stand up and, with deft strokes, lay bare the white meat of turkey breast and the dark meat of drumstick, and scoop out the dressing. Let no grim visage nor solemn discourse mar the pleasure of passing back for second helpings and then following these with cake and cookies, pies and strawberries. Finally, lay before Otis the steaming

Christmas pudding with its blue brandy flames flickering and following each other round and round about.

There's your recipe for Christmas dinner at Johnstone's — a boy's unforgettable Christmas dinner.

For hours afterwards Mother and Mrs. Johnstone washed dishes, and before they were all dried Lloyd and I were eyeing oranges and cracking nuts with a hammer. Soon Mrs. Johnstone dug out the ice-cream freezer; and this luxury, strange to a farm boy, would fill in any chinks that he developed as his enormous dinner settled. Then, as the early dusk dimmed the room, old man Johnstone brought out his fiddle and all joined in singing the old favourite songs — "My Old Kentucky Home," "Sweet Genevieve," "Kathleen Mavourneen," "Killarney," and many more. All the while Otis played the accordion and Lloyd chimed in with his Jew's-harp.

Finally the coal-oil lamps were lit, and Mrs. Johnstone began to prepare supper. But who, except the children, could eat any more? The adults had a cup of tea or coffee, and, for courtesy's sake, nibbled at some Christmas cake. The children, of course, did not miss the chance to start again; but, alas, as Mrs. Johnstone said, their eyes were bigger than their bellies. Sighs of satisfaction succumbed to sighs of surfeit, while heavy eyelids testified to the toll taken by Christmas. It was time to go home.

Chappie and Charlie were soon hitched up to the sleigh, and amid repeated shouts of "See you at New Year's!" they picked their way along the trail, winding through the twisted birches and the stark tamaracks. Bill and I were soon settled down in the bottom of the sleigh-box, while Dad and Mother sat watching the trail ahead as it wound into the recesses of the forest.

And so the team and sleigh slipped along the trail, leaving the great trees to stand sentinel all through the night. Then out across the big meadow the horses trotted, swinging around the shadowy willows whose flaring branches were dotted with a dozen partridges huddled into balls, asleep — inky silhouettes against the streaming Northern Lights. The horses quickened their pace as they came to the rise that marked the ascent to our clearing. Their heel chains fairly rang now that they were in sight of the smokeless house and the shadowy barn, and in a moment we were home.

Dad sprang out of the sleigh to unhitch the horses, glad of the exercise to revive chilled limbs. Mother climbed down carefully, and she and her two boys, mumbling with sleepiness, bumbled their way into the darkness and the chill of the farmhouse whose wood fires had gone out hours ago. She groped for the lamp and lit it. Soon, paper and kindling were piled on the fleecy grey ashes of the old air-tight heater. For a moment the match flickered, then caught the paper, and in minutes the fire was roaring away. I don't think that there is any kind of heater which warms an ice-cold room so quickly as these old-time ones. With hands nearly numb with cold you stood around and the very roar of the fire catching on the spruce logs seemed to warm you. As soon as the fire was well established and roaring up the smoke-pipe, you partially closed the damper in that pipe. At the same time you burned your fingers as you screwed in

the little damper low down on the front of the heater. The adjustment of these two dampers was always a delicate one, because if it was not done exactly right, the fire would start to puff like a locomotive, and billows of smoke and spurts of flame nearly rocked the heater off its legs. Glowing red spots soon appeared on the metal sides of the heater. Then it was time to take off your cap and coat, for soon the room would be too warm. A wonderful thing was on old air-tight heater.

Soon the chill was off the living-room of the MacGregor household, and before long it was time to go to bed. That takes a bit of courage too — leaving the fire and climbing into an ice-cold bed. For fifteen or twenty minutes the issue is uncertain. If you can stick it out long enough to warm the bed, you win, for the pile of blankets is a wonderful insulator; if you warm just that small part of the bed in contact with you, the blankets will keep the heat from escaping. Your face and nose, exposed to room temperature, may almost freeze, but never do. Soon you drop off to a blissful sleep.

Cranberry Sauce

This recipe, attributed to a Mrs. McLaren, comes from the High River Cook Book, *published by the Ladies Aid of Chalmer's Church in 1907.*

One and one-half quarts of cranberries, pressed through a colander, one and one-half quarts of chopped onions, two pounds of brown sugar, one and one-half tablespoonfuls of salt, one quart vinegar, one tablespoonful each of ginger, cloves, allspice and cinnamon. Boil until thick.

Christmas Fig Cake

Mrs. W. H. Todd's recipe for fig cake also appeared in the High River Cook Book.

One cup of butter creamed, one and one-half cups of sugar, one cup of milk, three cups of flour, three level teaspoonfuls of baking powder sifted with flour (sift flour three times), whites of four eggs; bake in two layers. Add to the remainder the yolks of two eggs, one-half cup each of raisins and currants, a sprinkle of sliced citron, one grated nutmeg, one-half teaspoonful each of cinnamon and cloves, two tablespoonfuls of molasses and one-quarter of a cup of flour. Bake in a tin the same size as other layers and put together with the following fig filling: Chop one pound of figs, add one-half cup of sugar and one cup of water, stew until soft and smooth. Spread between layers and ice the top with chocolate icing.

Christmas Stuffing

A mother with four school-aged children, Leta R. Porter wrote a number of poems which they could use as recitations at school Christmas concerts. The following one was written for "our chubby young son. He got it off well and created a big laugh." Because of its success, Mrs. Porter decided to share it with readers of the Farm and Ranch Review in 1930.

Christmas Recitations

I'll tell you a tale of a very small boy
   with an appetite large in proportion:
When Christmas time came he ate all he could hold,
   even ate to the state of distortion.
On turkey and pie and cranberry sauce,
   on pudding and cake and much candy,
With oranges, apples, popcorn and nuts,
   he stuffed on whatever came handy.

Now flesh has a limit; most folk will agree,
   though the spirit be ever so willing;
'Twas really surprising how one little boy
   could hold such a lot at one filling.
The night came at last; his endurance
   ebbed fast; the feasting and merriment ended.
Then came a suggestion of punishing pains
   in a tummy too tightly distended.
"Oh, Gee!" sighed the boy, "It's a whole
   year again, I must wait for what Santa will send me,
And Mother, I'm tired; so put me to bed.
   But whatever you do, don't BEND me!"

My Best Christmas

In 1910, the Grain Growers' Guide sponsored a contest among the children of their rural readers, to see who could write the best story about a Christmas they had experienced. The winner from more than 100 entries was twelve-year-old Doris Wright, of Boissevain, Manitoba. She received three dollars for this essay.

he best Christmas I ever spent started like this: When I emptied my stocking, I had breakfast and began to think what I should do for the day. First of all we thought we would go and skate (for it was a lovely day, crisp and sunshiny) but when we got down to the lake it was lumpy so we could not skate. We came in after a good game of snowball and we had dinner. We had duck and turkey, cranberry sauce, potatoes, turnips, mince pie and plum pudding, followed by candies, oranges and nuts, etc.

Then we thought we would spend the afternoon by going to visit a poor family where the mother was ill. We packed a basket with all kinds of food and we put some candies and toys and some fire-crackers in it for the little boys and girls; all of them were small. About one o'clock when everything was packed, dinner over, we put on our hats and coats and the team stood there in the double-seated sleigh and away we went taking with us our skates and the dogs running behind. I thought we might have some skating if the ice was good down there for it was a five mile drive and we thought they might not have had the same kind of a wind to make the ice lumpy, nor had any snow to freeze into it.

It was a beautiful drive and we were not a bit cold with robes to cover us and the bottom all covered with straw to keep our feet warm. We got there about half past two. When we went into the house there was a big fire but they had nothing to eat but a loaf of bread, because none of them were able to go to town and nobody passed that way. They brought the basket in and mother unpacked it. The mother was in a very poor condition and she had not had any food since morning. Mother gave her some of everything we had brought and we had a dandy time till supper playing games.

Before supper one of the boys went out to see the ice and said it was almost as clear as glass. After supper they hunted out their old skates and found enough for three and that was all that could go. There were six of us and three of them, so we made quite a crowd.

TOBBY IT, TOM.

Medicine Hat News,
December 20, 1894.

111

Christmas in the West

We went down there, and it was beautiful. We skated for about an hour in the moonlight and then went back to the house and on the way we sang a Christmas carol. We went to the house and warmed ourselves and then the boys got the team in the sleigh and we drove home and we never spent a jollier Christmas.

Reta, Charles, and Margaret Simpson were photographed with their Christmas tree at Yorkton, Saskatchewan in 1910. Their father, T. V. Simpson, was the local doctor. Note the stockings on the wall.

A Hard Times Christmas

Although the Great Depression did not arrive until the 1930s, many homesteaders knew about hard times long before that date. Some had little or no money as they tried to prove up on their lands; others suffered through the post-war recession which hit the West after 1918. In 1921, Amy J. Ross, the editor of "Women's Forum" for the Grain Growers' Guide, drew upon her own experiences to tell her readers how to "make do" at Christmas.

imes were hard and money was scarce, but I made up my mind to have a merry Christmas for the children in spite of everything. I got an idea out of a magazine that children's toys should be something that would keep them busy during the long winter days in the house, and not some bright, gaudy thing that would be broken up and useless in a week; and with this thought in mind I went to work.

I sent for some educational supply catalogs and pored over the Busy Work pages and the kindergarten material in order to get some definite suggestions.

The first item on my Christmas program was household decoration. There were garlands and a big bell from other years to be sure, but to be really merry there must be something new. I sent the children, always eager for some new task, to the haystack, where they selected a small armful each of big, firm, even wisps of hay. These they cut into one-inch lengths and put in an Old Chum box for safe keeping. Then began a search for bright colored papers. There was red off the tea and yellow off the mustard and cocoa cans, and bright advertisements from the magazines and catalogs, brown wrapping paper, too, and even some plain printed paper. All this was cut in one-inch squares and put in another box. Darning needles and cord came next, stringing first a square of paper, then a piece of hay and then another square, alternating the bright colored paper with the drab. Each child made a garland of his own to be put away in the trunk until the week would arrive and many happy thoughts were packed away with it to reappear with much laughter and fun when the day for hanging the decorations actually arrived.

But what about the presents? Vera was nine. She did want a little trunk to hold her fancy work, her sewing, her doll clothes, all the

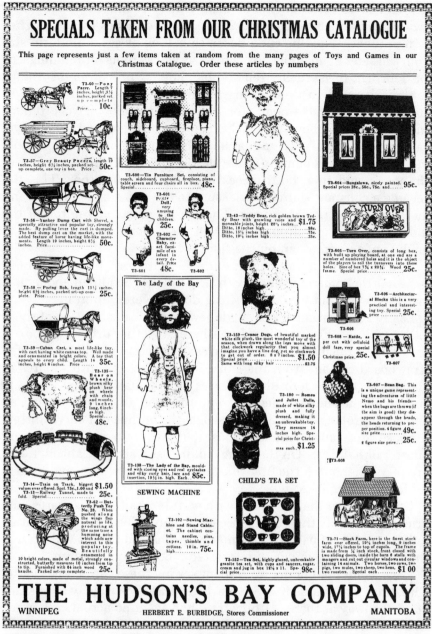

For the 1911 Christmas season, the Hudson's Bay Company selected items from its catalogue and advertised them in the *Grain Growers' Guide*. Note the special Bay doll with "closing eyes and real eyelashes and silky curly hair."

things dear to a little girl's heart. To buy one was out of the question, but Daddy came to the rescue and put a neat little cover on a wheat porridge box from the grocery. However, it did look lonesome and bare, so I hunted up some odds and ends of cloth and cut out some new clothes for Vera's doll, and put them inside. Vera was worrying too about a set of paper dolls, like Eileen Brown's. I managed to find some of these in an old magazine and pasted them on old, worn out muslin to make them substantial. When Christmas morning came my little lady was somewhat disappointed in her old box at first, but it looked better when all her treasures were stored away in it, and in the course of a few weeks she became very much attached to it.

Johnnie and Pearlie were five and three. Johnnie wanted everything he saw in the catalog, especially building blocks, erector

Facing page: Christmas was a time for children, even when pioneers had no money. The tree at the Gerding home near Vulcan, Alberta was sparsely decorated in 1917; and the dolls were repainted each year for the children.

The Jones Manufacturing Company of Winnipeg encouraged girls to sell Christmas booklets in 1911 to win this Parisienne doll.

sets and mechanical toys. For him, Daddy found an old piece of two-by-four which he cut into 24 blocks, two inches by four inches by four inches. Next he cut a dozen thin, long pieces of uniform size from the sides of an apple box. These served as roofs for buildings, or for fencing. It is really remarkable how many different things Johnnie learned to build. This finished, Daddy went to work to make an "over and under" for Johnnie's marbles. Two ordinary one-inch boards about two inches wide and a foot and a half long had a groove cut in each so that a marble would run down in. A hole was drilled big enough for a marble to drop through in one end of one piece, and then both pieces were fastened together. This toy became a constant source of pleasure to the two small children and the envy of the neighborhood. The marble starts at the top of the slide, runs down and drops through the hole on to the other slide and finally ends up in a pan on the floor.

Pearlie wanted a doll buggy; our substitute for which turned out to be a little home-made bed with tick, pillows, bed linen and a quilt made by Vera and a brand new rag dolly covered up in it.

Lastly I made some home-made sewing cards in imitation of those in the catalogs. For cardboard I gathered together dried fruit boxes, shoe boxes, raisin and currant boxes, soap cartons and some large strawboard cartons from the store. These were cut into squares or oblongs of three or four uniform sizes. On one half of them I drew in outline all the simple objects I could think of, an orange, a pear, an apple, a carrot, a potato, a cup, a sleigh, the outline of Pearl's mitten, a house, etc., and I pricked these outlines with a hat pin every quarter or half inch. On these the children sew straight ahead, filling in every other stitch the first time and going over it a second time to fill in the alternate stitches.

On the other half I drew with a ruler half-inch squares and pricked a hole at the corner of each square. These cards afford an infinite variety of patterns, for many designs and figures will present themselves to the minds of interested mother and children.

Long, contented hours were spent sewing these cards, weeks after Christmas had passed; even the little three-year-old was making good headway at them. Although we had spent no actual cash at all, this was voted one of the best Christmases the Ross family had ever spent.

Useful Christmas Gifts

In 1925, the Farm and Ranch Review had a contest to find out which readers could best describe how to make their own Christmas gifts. One of the winners, identified only as M.W., explained how an early winter had prevented her family from finishing the harvest, so money was in short supply. She presented the following suggestions for making Christmas gifts.

ith preparations for Christmas now only a matter of weeks away, the busy housekeeper turns her mind to gifts, which, this year, must of necessity be inexpensive, with so much of the grain unthreshed.

For making dainty and useful gifts, nothing will come in handier than sacks. Flour, sugar, cereal and salt sacks can all be sterilized. In the first place, to wash out the lettering, use Naptha soap and cold water. Afterwards, wash and iron like ordinary linens, and you have material for a surprising number of gifts.

A beautiful tablecloth can be made from four squares, put together with strips of colored cotton. Have the joining sections double so that all seams are inside. Put a double fold of the same material around the outer edges and both sides of the cloth will be the same. Any desired shade may be used. Delft blue is very pretty and durable.

A breakfast or tea cloth can be made from one square, blanket stitched around in red, blue or black, with a small pattern on one or more corners. A more elaborate cloth can be made with crocheted edge, and four or six serviettes with the same edge to match.

Perhaps no tea towel gives more worthwhile service than the one made from a flour sack. For gifts, they can be embroidered in simple stitch with such patterns as cup and saucer, knife and spoon, glass or pitcher.

Hot dish holders are always acceptable. Small squares interlined with clean, soft, worn cloth, and stitched from corner to corner, or in squares, make very pretty holders. Bind or blanket stitch the edges, and put a ring, loop or eyelet in one corner to hang them up by.

The large sized sugar sacks are best adapted for dusters, as they are so soft. Hemmed nicely and marked "Duster" with red or blue chain stitch, they find a ready welcome from many a friend.

For the children, the small salt sacks make pretty handkerchiefs.

117

Plain hem the edges and put an initial, a flower or a figure in one corner, or use a simple, easy crocheted edge. Slightly larger squares hemmed and marked "Noon House," or "Good Eats," make attractive cloths to place inside the school lunch basket, pail or kit.

A few other suggestions for useful articles would be, children's underwear (bloomers or slips), rompers, aprons, caps, kitchen curtains for the shorter windows, cushions, doilies, buffet or dresser covers. Any or all of these might be enhanced with facings of gingham or chambray, leftover from the summer dresses.

If the supply of sacks is limited, a few yards of unbleached cotton, at a very reasonable cost, may be used with the material on hand for these attractive, useful hand-made gifts.

Although Simpson's could not compete with Eaton's and the Bay for prairie trade, they did advertise their Christmas specials in western magazines. In this 1911 advertisement the company offered to pay for the shipping costs.

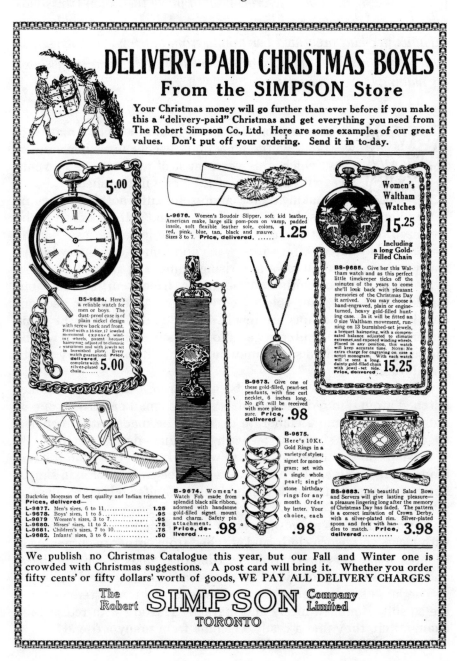

The Christmas Tree

Scandia is a small village on the broad, treeless plains south of Brooks, Alberta. Perhaps settlers there could get a Christmas turkey and presents, but to find a tree was another matter. This account is drawn from Scandia Since Seventeen, a local history.

he year was 1918 when two young men hauled three loads of wheat into Brooks and then went shopping to purchase their Christmas supplies. At that time Brooks had a population of about 200 and two stores, both of which sold only practical merchandise. The farm population between Brooks and the Bow River, 30 miles south, consisted of only eight people.

One of the young men had a wife and three children at home so he went looking for a Christmas tree. Since he and his family came from Minnesota, where there was a surplus of these trees, he was perplexed and upset when he could not find one. Eventually, he went to the CPR office to complain about the difficulty he was having trying to find a Christmas tree on the barren prairie, and to point out that he could not celebrate Christmas properly without one. In short, he accused the CPR of not looking after its settlers properly.

The next morning the two men got up at 4:30, fed and harnessed their horses, ate a cold breakfast and started off for home without the coveted tree. Since it was a very cold morning, they walked beside their wagon to keep warm.

About half way home, the man who had been looking for the tree jumped up on his wagon; then jumped off again just as quickly, shouting to his friend, "Why did you do it? Why did you do it?" The friend, not knowing what had happened, looked into the wagon and there on the bottom lay a beautiful four-foot green spruce.

Proudly the father took the tree home to his family. But the reception the tree received from his wife and children was disconcerting, to say the least.

They did not want it!

While he was away they had gathered a big bunch of Russian thistle, or tumble weed, placed it in the corner of their two-room home and decorated it with Christmas ornaments brought from Minnesota. So pleased were they with their novel decoration that they did not want a real tree. From then on, until local Christmas

Eaton's catalogue was the Bible of the western farmer, as indispensible in the home as in the outhouse. So well known was the catalogue that Eaton's did not need to itemize its wares in its magazine advertising, such as this 1919 example.

trees became readily available, the wives of all new settlers used gaily decorated Russian thistles for their Christmas trees.

But what of the Christmas tree that was laying on the bottom of the wagon? How did it get there? Several years after the incident, it was discovered that Augustus Griffin, the CPR's district engineer, had quietly cut down one of the hundreds of trees he had planted and placed it in the wagon of the young father from Minnesota.

J. A. Hawkinson was the father of the three children, and Carl Anderson was the other driver.

A card sent to the Werthenback family of Biggar, Saskatchewan in 1922, from friends in Minnesota.

May Christmas at your house in gladness abound And health and good cheer Live there all the year round

A MERRY CHRISTMAS

Ethnic Settlements

Norwegian Pioneers

When settlers came to western Canada from their homelands around the world, many brought their own Christmas customs with them. Some of these remained intact while others were adapted to the new frontier. Just as the Scandia settlers used tumbleweeds instead of Christmas trees, so did the early Norwegians adapt their customs to their simple homestead life. Authors Regna Steen and Magda Hendrickson describe the first Christmas of settlers in the Bardo district south of Tofield, Alberta.

 hristmas meant much to the people of Norway; it meant even more to the early Norwegians on this continent, for at Christmas more than ever, they remembered fondly and missed sorely the old home, relatives and friends.

Christmas was celebrated in the old country on a large and elaborate scale. Preparations began weeks and weeks before the great holiday. If possible, every member of the family must have new clothes and shoes at Christmas, or at least something new to wear. All these things were made at home. Flatbread ("flatbrød") had to be baked; beef and pork dressed; meat balls, sausage and ribs prepared, and pigs' feet pickled. The dry cod had to be soaked in a bath of lye, for Christmas without "lutefisk" would not be Christmas in a Norwegian home.

The house was scrubbed and washed from top to bottom. All clothing and bedding had to be washed or aired. Everything must be spick and span and clean-smelling. Then came the baking of "lefse", "fattigmand" (poor man's cake), "julekake", "gorobrød", and many tasty things to eat.

While the women were busy with all this, the men had to see to it that wood was split and put in neat piles and that kindling wood was plentiful and in its right place.

During all these weeks the very air was pulsating with excitement. This reached the climax when sheaves of grain had been fastened to a tall pole down by the barn — a feast for the birds — and not the least so when father or one of the sons brought into the house the green and fragrant Christmas tree.

At five o'clock in the afternoon of Christmas Eve all work must be finished and everybody washed and in his Sunday best. When the clock struck five, the bells began to chime in the church tower on a

The Swedburg children of Marchwell, Saskatchewan enlivened their first Canadian Christmas with music. The family came from Sweden.

distant hill. The men would take off their caps, the women fold their hands, and the children grew very quiet and looked wonderingly up into the faces of their elders, while the bells rang in the holy Christmastide.

We must not forget to state that the cattle were given extra soft bedding and an extra large portion of feed. The stable itself was somehow different Christmas Eve, for was not Jesus born in a stable and cradled in a manger?

Then the family sat down to the most bountiful meal of all meals during the whole year, but before they partook of it, they all sang a Christmas hymn and father read the old story about the shepherds who watched their flocks at night; about the songs of angels and the announcement of the birth of Jesus. Afterwards they gathered around the Christmas tree and sang sweet old hymns. Then the presents were distributed.

On Christmas day all were up early and every member of the family would, if possible, attend church services. The horses had bells which rang out merrily in the frosty air and sleigh would follow sleigh over hills and valleys and through forests of evergreen, to the church on the hill.

These were precious memories to the new settlers in 1894, and they felt very lonely. But Christmas is Christmas everywhere and they decided to make the most of their circumstances. They would at least have a Christmas tree for the children. We suspect they also

122

May love and hope and health unite
To make your Christmas glad and bright.

This card was part of
a sample book used by salesmen
traveling in western Canada in the
1890s.

thought of themselves. Some things could undoubtedly be bought in Edmonton, but though the town was sixty miles away, Mr. and Mrs. Peter Jevning, Mr. P. B. Anderson and Mr. Lars Johnson decided to drive over the newly blazed trail through the timber, over hills and lakes, to do some Christmas shopping.

After an adventurous trip, they arrived in Edmonton. Mrs. Jevning was the first woman of [the Bardo] community to shop in that town. There wasn't much to choose from, to be sure, but they returned home with candles and tissue paper, and a bag of apples. Then a tree was procured and given a festive appearance with the simple trimmings which had been bought or made.

The weather was mild that winter with just enough snow for sleighing. Christmas Eve they all gathered in Nels Jevning's log cabin, fourteen by twenty feet. A choir which had practiced especially for the occasion sang several songs, one of which was "Nu Er Julen Kommen." The children sang "Jeg Er Saa Glad Hver Julekveld," while they held hands and walked around the tree. These two songs have been sung at every Christmas ever since.

All the children either recited or sang. One little fellow was to sing "Jeg er liden men jeg vil" ("I am little but I want to"). But he did not want to. This boy later became Missionary Palmer Anderson of China.

The venerable Bersvend Anderson spoke tenderly and touchingly on the old but ever new message, "Peace on earth, good will to men." How comforting to know that they were not so far away but that a message from God could reach them!

After the program each person received an apple and there were also a few small gifts, much appreciated by the children. Then lunch was served. The two Mrs. Johnsons had baked "lefse" and Mrs. Anderson had brought the butter to spread them. Someone furnished coffee, another cake, and a most festive hour was enjoyed by all.

And while outside the stars shone brightly in the sky and the northern lights flashed in flowing and ever changing colors across the heavens, these God-fearing pioneers out in the wide open spaces of Alberta, Canada, celebrated their first Christmas in this community. The children who were present would never forget that wonderful evening in the new land.

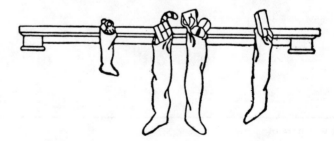

Men in Sheepskin Coats

Vera Lysenko's book Men in Sheepskin Coats, published in 1947, is considered to be a classic work in describing the experiences of the first Ukrainian settlers in western Canada.

or the first Christmas, the little clay houses were scoured clean; the children dressed in white skirts. The table was covered with hay, and a raisin cake covered with honey was put in a place of honour. Candles were lit, sheaves placed in the corners; incense burned through the house. At the decorated ikons the children knelt and prayed. Then the master of the house drew a straw and made a prediction of the abundance of crops according to the length of the straw. Before supper was eaten, the father exclaimed:

"Christ is born!"

And the women and children replied,

"Praise His Name!"

Then all sat down to supper of twelve dishes (for the twelve apostles), jellied fish, beans, plums, dumplings stuffed with cabbage or mushrooms, sour soup, herring, cheese, cabbage rolls, poppy seed cakes, meat pastries, buckwheat meal, and the sacred kutya of wheat, honey, nuts, poppy seed. If any of the family had died, there were spoons and bowls set for them at the table since the Ukrainians believe that the souls of the dead return at Christmas as guests to their homes and fly over the table to see if they are not forgotten.

Then the voices of carol singers were heard beneath the window, mingling grandeur and sorrow in a languishing melody:

O God Eternal, who in mortal language could utter
Your deep humiliation and your earthly incantation among us.

Then the carol singers wish happiness, luck and good harvest to those in the house and sing the magnificent carol:

All over the world there came the news
To Virgin Mary a son was born
On hay in the manger she laid the Son of God
Virgin Mary to God prayed, "In what should my
　Son be robed?"
O King of Heaven, send gifts through the master
　of the house.
Then came angels from heaven to earth, bringing gifts to the Virgin,

Christmas in the West

Three candles of wax and robes of silk for the
  infant in the manager,
In Jordan River, where quiet the water stood,
O there the Virgin Mother of the Holy Infant
  bathed him,
And when he was bathed, in robes of silk she robed him,
And when he was robed, in the manger she laid him.

Arthur Cunningham received this
card from a relative in Minnesota
about 1909.

An Icelandic Christmas

Saskatchewan author Walter J. Lindal describes the Christmas customs of Icelandic settlers in his province in the 1890s.

In Iceland, Christmas has always been a very religious festive holiday, in the word's original sense, although changes have taken place during the last half century in the capital and the larger towns and villages. Christmas Eve was Holy Night. All work was to stop at six o'clock, candles were lit, people, especially the children, put on their Sunday best. A joyous yet solemn evening was spent, befitting the sacred occasion.

The settlers in America continued this type of observance of Christmas. There were no gifts or Christmas cards but preparations had to be made for Christmas. For some time candles could not be bought and they were home-made. The neck of a bottle was used, a bottom made at the wider end and a grocery twine of proper size, substituting for a wick, was stretched taut from one end to the other; then hot tallow was poured in and after it cooled out in the snow the candle was pulled out ready for Christmas Eve.

At Christmas, even the very first years, there was some *baett brauð*, meaning pastry. There were the Icelandic specialties: *kleinur,* and *laufabrauð*, made out of doughnut batter; the famous *pönnukökur,* a very thin pan-sized pancake, spread with brown sugar and then rolled up and cut in two for serving. The Icelandic *Vinar-terta,* Vienna tart, of thin layers with prune filling, was rare during these early years. The delicacy in meat was smoked mutton, *hangikjöt,* which even yet is a favorite in Icelandic homes.

After the evening meal there usually was a brief service or a passage was read from the Bible. Then the final chores were done and about ten o'clock *Súkkulaði,* hot chocolate, was served.

One incident can be mentioned to illustrate how early and how deeply the religious side of Christmas was impressed upon the children. About five o'clock the children started to play and usually played until the evening meal was served. They formed a circle and in dancing around, sang some song their mother had taught them. On this occasion they sang *"Gamli Nói,"* "Old Man Noah," a ditty on a level slightly above a nursery rhyme. The first two lines are as follows:

> *"Gamli Nói, gamli Nói,*
> *guðhraeddur og vis."*

Peter Kuch

A girl watches her brother breaking off the top of a bottle to be used as a mould for making Christmas candles (ca. 1895).

Artist Peter Kuch shows how Icelandic children used the neck of a bottle to make a Christmas candle.

This is the view that greeted worshippers at the church of Saint Isidore de Bellevue at Bellevue, Saskatchewan, one Christmas eve' in the 1920s.

"Old man Noah, old man Noah,
God-fearing and wise."

The third and fourth lines in the second stanza are as follows:
*"Glappaskotin, glappaskitin,
ganga svo til enn."*
"All those errors, all those errors,
Happen even now."

The children were too young to understand all the words. The word *andskotinn* means the devil and is a common swear word in Icelandic and the children must have heard it. All at once it occurred to them that *skotin,* the second half of the word *glappaskotin* (which literally means "errors") was a swear word. To utter such a word on Christmas Eve was unthinkable. The children decided at once to skip that word in the second verse.

Here is an example of the endurance of the pioneers and at the same time reveals in a very striking way how important Christmas Eve was to the Icelandic people. Eirikur and Gudmundur Thorsteinson were the heroes of the event. They had been commissioned to go to Moosomin, a distance of thirty-three miles [from the Tantallon district], to get supplies for the approaching Christmas season. They travelled on foot as the oxen were needed at home. They bought a one hundred pound sack of flour, ten pounds of sugar, ten pounds of coffee, eighty-five pounds of rolled oats, and some special Christmas supplies such as chocolate, baking powder, etc. Eirikur carried the sack of flour, the coffee and sugar, and Gudmundur carried the rolled oats and the other Christmas supplies. With these loads on their backs the men walked the whole thirty-three miles!

128

Ham at seventeen cents a pound and sugar at a dollar for a fifteen pound bag seemed like reasonable prices in Medicine Hat in 1905.

Pönnuköhur

These Icelandic delicacies come from the kitchen of Marianna Wendel.

- 2 eggs
- ⅓ cup sugar
- ¼ tsp. salt
- ½ tsp. cinnamon
- ½ tsp. soda
- 1 tsp. baking powder
- ½ tsp. vanilla
- ½ cup sour cream or buttermilk
- 1½ cup flour
- 2 cups sweet milk

Beat eggs and add sugar, salt, vanilla, and cinnamon. Dissolve the soda in a little boiling water, mix with sour cream, and add to mixture. Add flour and baking powder sifted together. Beat well and gradually stir in the sweet milk. To fry use a crepe pan. Heat and rub with butter, then pour about ⅕ cup batter on it. Tip pan around until entire bottom is covered. Set back on high heat as quickly as possible, then turn and fry on other side. Stack in a pile, sprinkle with sugar or fold with jam and whipped cream. Makes about 26 cakes.

Vinarterta

- 1 cup butter or margarine
- 2 cups granulated sugar
- 1 cup brown sugar
- 3 eggs separated
- ½ cup whole milk
- 5 cups flour
- 3 tsp. baking powder
- 1 tsp. baking soda
- 1 tsp. cardammon
- 1 tsp. lemon flavouring
- 1 tsp. almond flavouring
- 1 tsp. vanilla
- 2 lbs. prunes (soaked overnight)

Mix first 12 ingredients together using only 1 cup of the granulated sugar. Divide dough into seven parts and pat onto baking sheets. Bake at 450°F, or less, until golden. Put layers together with prune filling between. Cut in small squares.

Prune filling: Boil prunes in enough water to cover them, cool, pit, mash, and put back on stove. Bring to boil with 1 cup granulated sugar and part of the water the prunes were boiled in. The mixture must be like thick jam.

Laufabrauð

- 2 lbs. flour
- 1½ tsp. baking powder
- 1 tsp. salt
- 4 qts. milk
- oil for deep frying

Boil the milk. Put the flour on the table and mix with salt and baking powder. Pour the boiling milk over it gradually and mix well. Knead dough until it is glossy and without any cracks. It should not stick to the table and the dough should be tough and solid. Shape into rolls which are divided into equal pieces. Roll the pieces in the palms of the hands to form even cakes that are spread out as thin as possible. The cakes should be round in shape and about the size of a small platter. All kinds of patterns are carved into the cakes with a knife. The cakes are then deep-fried in hot fat until light brown.

This is mainly a North Icelandic dish. It is usually made before Christmas and all members of the family gather together to carve patterns into the cakes.

Holidays for an English Settler

Kathleen Redman Strange, a well-known English-born author, describes the Christmas of 1920, her first in the West. The family farm was near the tiny whistlestop of Fenn, south of Stettler, Alberta.

t was almost Christmas, and still we had no house. It looked, indeed, as if we should have to spend Christmas Day in the shack.

All the time we had been sleeping in unheated granaries, and all the time it had been getting colder and colder. We had been driven at last into one granary, Harry and I sleeping in one bed and the three small boys in another. But even with a newly acquired stove, into which we thrust wood at frequent intervals throughout the bitter nights, mountains of blankets, and with a variety of dogs and cats piled on top of us for additional warmth, it was no uncommon occurrence to wake up literally stiff with cold in the morning and to find a rim of ice along the edge of the sheets where our breath had congealed during the night, and a layer of snow, sifted in through the cracks in the roof onto the bed-covers.

Our experiences were really mild when compared to those which most of our neighbors had gone through in earlier years. We knew that. But the knowledge that other people have suffered even greater physical discomforts and hardships than you yourself is precious little consolation to you when you are in the midst of suffering.

On the 23rd of December, our second wedding anniversary, Harry and I decided to discharge the remaining carpenters and move into the uncompleted house.

It was not a particularly attractive-looking place, either inside or out. The walls were bare white plaster, cold and cheerless-looking. The woodwork was unstained; so were the floors. There was no staircase, for the carpenters had not progressed to the making of one, and for several weeks after moving in we were obliged to use the kind of make-shift ladder affair which they had left behind. Its sudden collapse one day, with a very stout lady visitor aboard, induced us forthwith to engage the services of a carpenter who had received his training in the Old Country and who we judged would do the finishing work in good style.

As an initial experiment we kalsomined the walls in pastel

shades — a blue bedroom, a cream bedroom, and a green and pink one respectively. The living-room was rose and cream, and the kitchen buttercup yellow.

The woodwork everywhere, excepting in the kitchen where it was enamelled white, was stained a dark oak and waxed and polished. Last of all we scraped, varnished and polished the floors till they shone like the good hardwood they were not.

A hot-air furnace and storm doors and windows ensured us adequate warmth. Of course, one suffered a bit from lack of fresh air, but I have never been the proverbial fiend for fresh air that most of my compatriots have the reputation for being, so I soon got used to it. Indeed, colds were rare in wintertime, despite these conditions, and we usually all enjoyed good health.

It seemed at first as if we were going to see the unusual phenomenon of a green Christmas. Although the weather had been exceedingly cold on occasion, there had been very little snow.

On Christmas morning, however, we woke up to find the ground covered deeply with snow. The countryside at last presented a seasonable aspect.

As Christmas Day itself approached, I had been wondering how we would spend it. Here we were, on a lonely Western farm, many thousands of miles from relatives and friends who might otherwise have shared it with us. Back in England it had always been such a lovely day; a time for family reunion, for gifts and good wishes and for all the happy festivities associated with the season. There had always been church on Christmas morning — a bright and cheerful service in a gracious old church gaily bedecked with holly and evergreens, and this had always been followed by a traditionally

Mother would have loved an asbestos-lined kitchen range for Christmas, particularly if she had only a tiny wood stove. This advertisement appeared in the *Grain Growers' Guide* in 1911.

large dinner that seemed to last for hours, and then games and fun that continued for the best part of the night.

But here in this strange country of Canada it promised to be a very different story. For one thing, there would be no Christmas service. The minister had notified us that he would not be coming out. The house itself was far from attractive. How to give such an uninviting-looking place a real Christmas atmosphere?

After scouting around a bit on the farm, we had finally found a solitary fir tree in a coulee, which we cut down and brought carefully home. Some of the branches were trimmed off and used for decorating the living-room. We had sent to town for some tinsel and coloured paper, and with this we decorated the tree and the room as artistically as possible. We eschewed candles, for there was too much danger of fire with them. Our furniture — what we had of it — was well polished up, and we made the best of it by bringing out of our trunks some of our wedding-presents — pieces of silver and fine linen, somewhat incongruous in that barren setting, I admit, but guaranteed to remind us that there were better days to come.

The living-room, after we had finished with it, didn't look at all bad. On the broad mantel above the fireplace we had set out most prized possessions — a couple of hand-carved Chinese vases made from fine old koa-wood; a brass ship clock that had been rescued from an American warship that had been driven ashore at Samoa in a great gale and presented to my husband by its captain who had fortunately been saved; and an old brass inkstand that had been in the family since the time of Bishop Latimer, to whom it had originally belonged, and from whom, on my mother-in-law's side, my husband was directly descended. We brought in stout logs and burned them on the open hearth. They let out a fine, tangy smell and sparked and crackled in the most friendly fashion imaginable.

A few days before Christmas I had to set to baking the puddings and making the mincemeat. What a business it was, getting that pudding ready. I tried hard to remember how my mother had made hers. I had one of her treasured recipes with me and I followed it with the most meticulous care. I had to remember that candied peel must be sliced, not chopped; that suet must be chopped, not mashed up. That eggs must be broken one by one into a dish. My mother had always said: "One stale egg will spoil the whole pudding!"

When it was all put together, the mixture had to be well stirred. The three small boys took a hand in this, the hired men, too. Each one twirled the big wooden spoon and made a wish. At last it was all in the cloth and ready to be popped into the pot. So far, so good. But how would it turn out?

Every day, the week before Christmas, we had driven into town to see if any parcels had arrived from home. But beyond a few cards from scattered friends, there was nothing. The day before Christmas even the trains didn't turn up. We felt that every man's hand was against us indeed.

We had tried very hard to find at least one extra person to spend Christmas Day with us. But at first it seemed as if there was no one who did not have a place to go. Not that we did not appreciate one another's company, and would have been happy enough by ourselves anyway, but because we had always felt that we must follow the approved English custom of extending good cheer and good will at Christmas time by inviting some stranger to share our Christmas feast with us.

At the last moment, however, we had two guests instead of one. Our neighbor asked us if he might come over. His wife had been called down to the States on account of illness in her family, and he was unexpectedly left all alone. He arrived just before dinnertime on Christmas Day, bringing with him a veritable avalanche of parcels which he had picked up that morning at the railway station. The two trains, it appeared, had gone through during the night, and so we got our Christmas gifts in good time after all.

Our guest had also picked up the elevator man from Fenn, genial Dick Graham, one, by the way, who represented a class of man who plays a very important part in the social and economic life of Western Canada. Dick handled, graded and purchased practically all the grain in our community that went to market in those days. He was the connecting link between the wheat market of Winnipeg and the farmers on the plains. Prices came through him, and many a valuable tip he gave us about farming and the management of horses and stock. He was always ready with help and advice, whenever it was required, and was a most popular addition to all parties and social functions.

The co-operative movement could never tear itself away from politics, not even at Christmas, as indicated by this 1909 cover for the *Grain Growers' Guide*.

135

Christmas in the West

Among our Christmas gifts we found one from the Old Country that gave us particular pleasure and delight. This was a "wireless set" — a home-made radio, constructed by a radio engineer in London who was a friend of ours. From it we managed to get the most remarkable results. Not only were we successful in tuning in on stations all over Canada and the United States, but we actually managed to connect up with London itself.

Our little radio set consisted of three tubes in a simple wooden box, and three sets of earphones — a most primitive-looking contrivance when compared to present-day luxurious models of workmanship and design. Yet how we enjoyed it. People came from far and near to listen in to it. For many years it was the only radio within a radius of many miles, and we were kept busy by neighbours who called to know the latest weather reports and grain prices and the news of the day that came to us regularly over the air.

Our first Christmas dinner! What heart-burnings I suffered during the course of its preparation. Supposing the turkey should not be properly done inside? The mince pies burned? The pudding all tumbled to pieces when it was turned out? The crucial moment arrived at last — the moment for dishing up. I was almost in tears. Foolish, perhaps, to get so upset over such trifles, yet many others have shed tears, I have no doubt, over similar trifles before.

To my intense surprise and relief, despite all the alarms and excursions that had occurred during the morning, the dinner turned out a success after all. The turkey was plump and young; it was done to a turn. The stuffing was tasty — by a miracle I had put in just enough onion and not too much. Everyone came back for more. As for the pudding, it came out of its cloth without the loss of so much as a single crumb. I put a sprig of holly on top of it. Naturally I wanted to serve it in the good old English way. The lighted pudding had always been a great event of my own young days. One of the hired men, who had followed me into the kitchen seeing me with the brandy bottle in my hand, asked me what I was going to do with it. "I'm going to pour some over the pudding and set fire to it," I told him. "Will you please cut me a slice first?" he asked. "You see, I 'm a strict teetotaler."

I cut a piece for him, but omitted to tell him that there was a quarter of a pint of brandy inside the pudding itself.

When the dishes were finally washed and put away, I joined the group around the fireside. Daylight was fading, the curtains were drawn, the lamps lit. The fire blazed merrily. Everyone appeared to be in a mellow mood, satisfied and happy.

For the first time since leaving home and loved ones I felt happy myself. After all, I had now established a home of my own. I had a new generation of loved ones around me. Even if this was not the place where I had really wanted to be, even if I was still unsettled, still feeling a bit like a fish out of water, at least the worst of the rough edges had now been worn off and the future promised a little smoother sailing.

I have spent many happy Christmases since but never one that was any happier than that first Christmas on the prairies.

136

The Christmas specials offered by Columbia Records in 1916 ranged all the way from carols to Al Jolson.

These whimsical woodcuts appeared in the *Winnipeg Sun* on December 31, 1883.

Now the New Year was approaching. How were we going to celebrate that?

I decided to make it the occasion of a house-warming and invited some thirty of my neighbours to a dance. Our music was to a be a fiddle and a guitar.

Five of the thirty I had invited sent word to say they could not come. Would not, is perhaps more correct, since they belonged to the non-dancing element and most emphatically did not approve of the form my party was to take. That left twenty-five prospective guests and for them I made my plans.

The night of the dance broke stormily. Heavy clouds gathered in the sky, a cold wind whistled in from the north, and the thermometer dropped many degrees below zero.

But this did not deter my guests. Far from it. By eight o'clock they began to arrive. Singly, in couples, and in parties. The yard slowly began to fill up with sleighs, cutters and saddle horses, which were tethered to every available fence post and every handy tree.

People came in at the front door, at the back door, and at the side door. They came in so thick and fast that I gave up any attempt to welcome them, hostess fashion, but allowed them to crowd me into a corner while they filed past, up the stairs and into all the bedrooms, there to deposit their wraps and their sleeping babies on the beds — the babies, to my subsequent amazement, for the most part sleeping soundly all night, heedless of the constant babble of voices, the shuffling of innumerable feet, and the incessant scraping of fiddles.

Actually about eighty people turned up at that party, the majority of them being perfect strangers to me. Some of them came from twenty and thirty miles away. Word of the dance had travelled far and wide; every one wanted to come and have a good look at me, at my family, and at my new house. My invitations, I found, had really been superfluous. If you give a party in the country, then you must expect any one and every one who hears about it to come.

When the big living-room was literally jammed with people, the orchestra started to play. One of the crowd appointed himself a sort of master-of-ceremonies, and shouted out the various numbers, which, as usual, followed each other in breathtaking succession. The floor soon began to heave so alarmingly that we had to dash down into the basement, find a substantial post, and prop it up for safety. In less time that it takes to tell, the entire surface was gone from my carefully polished wood, and many hours of hard labour had been completely wiped out.

When the supper hour approached I went into the kitchen, in some trepidation, to see about the refreshments. I had prepared for twenty-five people. How was I ever going to feed this large and probably hungry multitude? To my surprise I found the room already in possession of a group of farm women who seemed to have taken charge of proceedings. The brimming wash-boiler was set on the stove and was emitting the pleasing aroma of boiling coffee. My plates of sandwiches and cakes had been brought forth from the cupboard and were set out in readiness on the kitchen cabinet.

"I'm sure there isn't enough to go round," I deplored, looking

138

anxiously at the now meagre appearing display. "There are so many more people than I expected."

"Oh, you don't need to worry," one of the women assured me. "There's tons of food." She pointed to the kitchen table, on which, I now noticed for the first time, were piled a number of bulky looking packages.

"What — is that food?" I asked.

"Yes. Didn't you know that everyone brings something along to a party like this. You surely didn't expect to have to feed all this crowd yourself?"

"Well, I didn't expect to feed quite so many," I admitted. "This seems to be a splendid idea, though."

There turned out to be sufficient eatables to feed almost twice the number of people who were present. In fact, we lived on sandwiches and cakes for days afterwards. And what delectable sandwiches and cakes they were, too.

It was not until about four o'clock in the morning that the apparently still-unwearied orchestra finally broke into the strains of Home Sweet Home and the crowd began reluctantly to gather together their babies and their belongings and set out for home.

The earlier hint of a storm had by this time developed into a lively blizzard, and the snow was coming down so thick and fast that it was almost impossible to see more than a foot or two ahead.

Some of our guests started out bravely enough but got no farther than our nearest neighbour's house, where they had to remain till the storm let up, many hours later. Others breasted it to their own doors, but reported a terrible trip. A large number decided to remain right with us until the worst was over. They were there for breakfast and some even stayed till dinnertime.

Mince Meat

A Winnipeg publication, Bulman's Farm and Motor Magazine, *published this recipe in 1910.*

Get two pounds of beef — many use neck beef — and cook it until the meat is very tender, then chop it fine and add the same bulk of chopped tart apples, one pound of seeded raisins, one pound of currants, a cupful of cooked cranberries, sugar sufficient to sweeten, chopped citron, one pint of raspberry juice, and spices finely ground and made to suit the taste. Add enough good cider vinegar to mix all ingredients and pack into a stone jar one week before using. The cider preserves the mince meat, which, if kept cool, will last a long time and a large amount can be made at one time and fresh pies baked when needed. One can add suet if it is desired, but most persons use cider. If apples are scarce use cranberries.

Christmas Plum Pudding

This recipe appeared in the same 1910 issue of
Bulman's Farm and Motor Magazine.

An old English recipe. (Will keep indefinitely.) 1 lb. of
suet, 1 lb. of raisins, 1 lb. of currants, half a pound of flour,
half a pound of bread crumbs, 1 lb. mixed orange, lemon and citron
peel (chopped), juice of one lemon, ½ lb. of sugar (white),
1 teaspoonful of salt, 1 nutmeg, 8 eggs, ¼ lb. almonds (pounded
and blanched), 1 tumbler (small) of brandy. Mix all together with
beer or stout, let stand for 12 hours, then boil for 9 hours; then
boil for 6 hours the day you use. Three times the quantity will make
six puddings.

In 1913, this card was sent to Otto
Dempsey, in Imperial,
Saskatchewan by his brother
Stuart in Young, Saskatchewan.

140

Country Schools

Behind the Sateen Curtain

An important center for community social activities was the school-house, and the Christmas concert was the highlight of the winter season. Writing for The Country Guide and Nor'-West Farmer in 1936, Margaret Parker describes such an event.

The school, in the four or five days before Christmas eve, forsakes its strictly utilitarian character to become the stamping-ground of high romance, when teacher and pupils "put on" their Christmas concert.

To be in a properly receptive mood for such a function, one should journey to the schoolhouse in a bobsleigh containing about a dozen passengers, behind a fat and frisky team shaking their bells over several miles of snowy road under the frosty stars. In the school, improvised seats of heavy planks laid upon thick up-ended fire-logs await the audience. The room has been cleaned and polished to an unusual degree. The "spitballs" with which some unregenerate spirit expressed his boredom with Long Division last September have been cleared from the ceiling. The map of Europe which won't roll up, and the map of northern Africa which has parted from its moorings have been summarily corded into place, and keep truce under a spray of paper holly. Every blackboard is adorned by drawings and stencils in passionate reds, greens and blues. A fine spruce towering in a front corner makes the big room fragrant. And behind the sateen curtain which conceals the stage, between two blanket-walled dressing-rooms, is heard a patter of hurrying feet, a rustle and thud of assembling "props," a sound of excited whispers.

Gentle reader! Have you ever transformed a very tangible little mortal into a fairy by the ruffly magic of crepe paper and tinsel? — or fitted the flowing cheesecloth robe and graceful wire-poised wings of an angel to the shoulders of an excitedly squirming young sinner? Have you ever, out of couch throws, table covers, and sundry borrowed "mufflers" garbed Joseph and the Shepherds for the Christmas pageant? or even, with the aid of a few rolls of crepe paper, two barrel hoops, a resurrected corset steel and a tableau light, evolved a loathsome dragon, spewing out fire and brimstone? If you have, you will have an idea of the thrills and perplexities amid which "teacher" has prepared for this important night!

Medicine Hat News,
December 20, 1894.

141

Christmas in the West

The school children are attired in all their glory. They shine with scrubbing and brushing — the boys in their "good pants" and sweaters, the girls in hand-made curls, silken bows and new dresses in a rainbow of color — for this is the great event of their year. It seems a pity to mar such festive array. But the items on the program must succeed each other without delay, so Peter Rabbit is put into his overalls, his eared cap and his big shoes, the "robins so red" don their brown-paper wings, and the daffodils their yellow ruffles in readiness for the play which follows the first chorus.

The seats in the schoolroom have been filled long since, and now an impatient burst of hand-clapping sounds outside the curtain. The teacher has a hurried word with the board member who is to act as chairman. His watch points to seven, the zero hour. There is a confusion of hurrying feet on the platform, then a sudden hush. The chairman steps up in front of the curtain and opens the program.

The teacher has optimistically headed the program with "address by the chairman," and now she is fervently hoping that it will be a real address, for the Joneses are late as usual, and Mary Jones must be in costume for the first play. But no — the chairman tells that ancient joke which avers that the best thing a chairman can talk about is — about two minutes, and announces the opening chorus. The curtain parts at last, revealing every child in the school — except the Joneses, alas! — singing "O, Canada!" with a gusto, at least, that leaves nothing to be desired. As the last stanza begins, the

The Moline School at Rapid City, Manitoba was decorated for Christmas in the 1890s by the local Patrons of Industry in preparation for the school play.

142

Joneses appear, and squirm through the crowded aisles to the dressing-rooms. Mary is rushed into her costume as Peter Rabbit's mother as the chairman announces the first play. Her eared cap has been knocked from the shelf by the out-filing "chorus," and there is a hasty search. She dashes to her place on the stage as the curtain parts, and the teacher sees too late that the wire in one of the ears has slipped, allowing the ear to dangle, which gives the Rabbit Mother an indescribably rakish appearance. However, she goes into her lines serenely. There are one or two minor hitches in the play. The daffodils forget their two lines — a contingency foreseen by the teacher, and the reason why, since every child must be given a "part" perforce, these three players had been made daffodils! But Peter Rabbit successfully evades the lady who wishes to put him into a pie, and the curtain closes amid applause.

A tall sophomore, home for the holidays, at a discreet hint from his proud family to the teacher, has been asked to give a reading. At its close, he is encored, and gives them Simple Simon, impersonating a small boy, with all the tricks of the elocutionist. As he retires, the chairman says, "We will now have a recitation by a beginner, Johnnie Smith." Six-year-old Johnnie scarcely waits for the announcement. Bounding upon the stage, he cries tearfully, gesturing after the departing collegian with indignation and despair: "He said my piece! he said my piece!"

So the "concert" goes on. Arthur Higgins, good steady fellow, plods through his long reading without missing a word — and almost without varying a tone. His mother in one of the front seats beams complacently around her, and comments, "seventeen verses, my dear!" to a companion in a triumphant stage whisper. Saint George in tinfoil struts his little hour upon the boards; the fairies go through their "bubble dance" with all the airy abandon of apple dumplings.

But at last the final chorus is sung. The costumes are all dropped into the capacious pasteboard box, and the performers, clad in their Christmas finery again, albeit a trifle wrinkled and awry, cluster upon a front bench. The chairman says that he is sure that Santa Claus will soon be here. Two or three of the school board go out — to look for Santa, the little girls think, though the older ones smile knowingly. The chairman remarks that he hopes Santa hasn't got his sleigh stuck in those big snow-banks over north in the woods. The smaller children turn pale.

Two minutes more of dreadful waiting, then — there is a jangle of sleighbells at the door, and Santa Claus — red-suited, rubicund, with the reddest of cheeks and the most fabulous of white whiskers — comes in, bending under the weight of a huge sack of apples and candy-bags. He calls out greetings, capers about with his bells jingling, then distributes the presents from the laden tree. Wonderful old Santa! — How well he remembers each child's name! He even knows that the Jones boys have a new little brother since last Christmas. What jokes he cracks! He pretends that the big packet for Buck Fisher is from someone whose name begins with "M" (though there's no sign of a name on it) just as if he knew that

143

Innisfail children, dressed for their Christmas pageant at the local Anglican Sunday School, posed with Santa Claus after the show. The event took place in Byron's Opera House in 1922.

Buck and Maisie Martin are to be married in February. He gives little girls the most fearful thrills by shaking hands with them; he slaps staid fathers on the back; he even sings a song in that muffled, mysterious voice of his. But all too soon it is over. He wishes everyone a merry Christmas, and whisks out of the door — where the reindeers of course, are waiting for him.

There is a pause in the merriment. At the suggestion of the Chairman an old carol is sung, then the national anthem. Neighbors part with noisy good wishes — and the Christmas concert is over for another year.

How to Make a Santa Claus Costume

When it came to making costumes, Mrs. E.F. Ashby believed in getting down to basics, including finding a wild rabbit to provide the fur trimming. The author lived on a farm south of Edmonton.

To make a Santa Claus costume is quite easy, inexpensive and creates endless fun. Moreover, if it is well made it will last for years and may be used at various Christmas festivities. You will need five yards of bright, sport red flannel, which costs 40 to 70 cents a yard, depending on the quality of the goods, half a dozen large white buttons, two spools of scarlet thread, and a small bottle of LePages glue. The fur trimmings and whiskers may be had for the making.

Let us first make the fur trimmings. On our farms are wild rabbits which are now turning white. The men folk must supply us with seven good skins which have been carefully removed and stretched over wooden frames to dry. When dry, they may be tanned, or, if clean and free from fat and meat, may be used as they are, for the costume is used only once a year and little actual wear takes place. Trim off the ragged edges (the tail and legs) and with a sharp knife carefully cut the skin into a long strip 2½ to 3 ins. wide. This is done by starting at the bottom and working round and round in a spiral to the top. Six good skins will trim the garments, and one good skin makes the collar.

Our old grey mare contributed the whiskers from her nice white mane. Everybody helps to make Christmas a success, and one must sometimes call in the aid of our animals as well. My faithful collie gave the mustache from his beautiful white collar. Doll's hair is merely stuck on with glue. We will do the same with the whiskers. As Dad might object to our sticking the whiskers on his face, we must make a mask on which to glue them. His chin and cheeks are covered with a piece of brown paper, over which is drawn a piece of cloth on the bias and fastened on top of the head. Loose parts of cloth should be drawn together with a needle and thread, making a snug fit all around. Now, take a soft lead pencil and mark out the area to be covered with the whiskers. This should extend from in front of the ears down around the chin, but need not extend much around the throat. The mask is now removed and placed around something as nearly the shape of the face as possible. We used a

145

Participants in the 1915 Sunday School Christmas concert at Nanton, Alberta posed on the stage at the Methodist church.

rather bottomed jug on which the mould was placed. The hair from the mare's mane is carefully removed with a pair of shears, the butts of the hair being kept together in as compact form as possible. Take a liberal supply of glue and smear the point of the chin well, then a tuft of the longest hair is carefully placed in position, the butts of the hair being well imbedded in the glue just as though growing there. If properly supported several tufts may now be placed in position and allowed to dry undisturbed. Continue to build it up step by step, a little now and then during the evenings, placing the longest tufts at the bottom, gradually working upwards until the ears are reached where the shortest tufts are placed.

Finish with a little of the finer dog's hair. Rough edges are carefully trimmed off where the cloth shows. Holes are cut for the ears. A piece of garter elastic is sewn on the top to securely hold it in place.

The mustache must now be made in the same way. A piece of cloth, the width of the upper lip and long enough to reach to the ear lobes is stitched onto a piece of garter elastic and placed in position over and behind the head, where it is securely held in place. When ready, this mustache is put on first, then the beard covers up the supports.

The coat is very simple. It is not going to be worn every day, and the looser it is, the better. A man's dressing gown, or a pattern of one, may be used as a guide. More than one man may use it so cut the goods plenty large enough.

Any odd pieces may be stitched together to form a cap or toque. A piece 24x26 inches will do nicely. Stitch the fur along one edge and turn up; then run up the seam, leaving the top open. Gather up the top about three inches from the end and securely fasten. Now cut the remaining three inches into strips to form a tassel. Put the cap on and suitably arrange and stitch the tassel to one side. Pull-over stockings may be made from other odds and ends if it is desired to hide the legs.

146

Christmas Consolation

This is the second of Leta R. Porter's poems, (the first is on page 110); this one was written in 1930 as a recitation for her six-year-old daughter.

I'd like to visit Santa Claus and play with
 all the toys
I'm sure I'd find just heaps of things to
 make a lot of noise.
I'd like to play with all the dolls and games,
 and Teddy bears,
And dolly carriages, and beds, and little
 rocking chairs.
But since he lives too far away for me to
 go, I fear,
I'm thankful, that at least he comes to
 visit me, each year.

Christmas Day 1893 —
— Calgary Canada —

Town and City Life

A Christmas Romance in Real Estate

At the time this incident occurred, Charles Lewis Shaw was a lawyer in Winnipeg. As a raconteur, he changed the names of the principals but the story is basically true. Certainly the real-estate boom was a fact of history. Shaw later joined a group of boatmen who went to Egypt for the relief of Khartoum and became a foreign correspondent. When he wrote this article in 1910, he had returned to Canada and was editor of the Edmonton News.

n the winter of 1881-82, the boom year of Winnipeg's history, St. John Selwyn was in the real estate business. His chief distinction — for almost everybody in Winnipeg at that time was either in the real estate or hotel business — rested on the fact that he pronounced his Christian name in arrogant English defiance of the Canadian rules of pronunciation. He was therefore called "Jack", as the name "Sinjin" required too much thought in those quick-moving days.

Mr. Selwyn made a very good real estate agent. He had become possessed of the idea that Winnipeg was going to be larger than Chicago in ten years. Up to the spring of 1882 that was one of the most profitable ideas a man in the real estate business could carry around with him. A man chuck full of that idea and one thousand dollars within reach could do very well during the winter of 1881-82.

That was the situation when Mr. Selwyn and a girl arrived at an understanding about one o'clock on Christmas morning, 1881. They were returning over the frozen Red River from attending midnight mass in St. Boniface cathedral and the girl's father and younger sister had been permitted to walk a considerable distance ahead of the couple, as had been the way since the beginning of time.

The hour, the season, the influence of the grand ritual of half an hour before, the quiet charm of the snow-clad scene, the glowing beauty of the fur-encompassed face, and the silence of the northern moonlight, all had their effect on the usually reticent young Englishman, for he told her the old, old story that is ever new to young lips and ears. It was difficult for any good-looking young Englishman with a well-modulated voice and all the stage-settings and atmosphere appropriate to the occasion to tell such a story badly and she whispered "Yes".

Facing page: Mrs. George Bruce and her three children sat outside their Calgary home on a cold Christmas morning to pose with their gifts. The children's uncle, Robert Randolph Bruce, was a creative photographer.

BILL OF FARE

AT THE

MANITOBA CLUB,

THIS DAY.

PEA SOUP,
Taken ready-made from the Red River.

DRIED SUCKERS,
Caught since the late election.

STEWED PEMMICAN,
Garnished with Buffalo hair.

DRIED MEAT,
On toast, served without knives and forks.

DESSERT.
Hudson's Bay Co. Rum and Pickles.

FRUIT.
Dried Apples.

The above is considered high-toned.

Poking fun at the elitist Manitoba Club, the *Winnipeg Quiz* devised this Christmas menu in 1878.

When the events on the ice of the Red River were hesitatingly and in part reported to Major Semple, the girl's father, the somewhat choleric half-pay officer flew into a characteristic rage and talked about "presumptious and beggerly" younger sons and forbade on pain of his deepest displeasure the slightest semblance of an engagement. And poor, pretty Marion Semple grew sad-eyed and St. John Selwyn fumed and smoked and drank more than was good for a man — even if he stood five feet eleven, measured forty-one inches about the chest, and wore only a six and three-quarter hat.

When Major Semple retired from a line regiment in the British army in the early 70's, he mistook the gambling spirit in his make-up for the business instinct. He came to Canada to make his fortune; he would then return "home" and enjoy a competence instead of eking out a shabby existence on half-pay and a meagre private income. He said pompously that he owed it to his family, but after a dozen ventures in all sorts of enterprises in eastern Canada, from agriculture on an Ontario bush farm to an agency for Ceylon tea and coffee in Montreal, the people he owed were not limited by any means to the Semple family. He then came west where nearly half a continent divided him from his creditors.

The boom of 1881 came as wine to the fevered lips of the drunkard to Major Semple. He felt that the opportunity of his life had come at last.

The sanguine major knew as much about real estate values or the probable growth of western Canada as a ten-year-old child. He mortgaged his pension up to the hilt, borrowed from every relative and friend that couldn't resist the fervent glow of his wide correspondence and by Christmas, 1881, he had an equitable title to redeem a large and varied assortment of real estate, sprinkled not only throughout the McPhillips survey of Winnipeg, but in every townsite that Jim Coolican and Joseph Wolf sold from alluring maps that showed market squares and city halls where the blooms lay undisturbed and untrampled.

At the Christmas tide of 1881, Major Semple was, in the parlance of the day, "loaded to the neck" with real estate and talked complacently about selling out some day when his property reached its real value of a quarter of a million dollars.

In January and February, 1882, there became noticeable in Winnipeg a decided lull in the storm of speculation that had attracted the attention of the civilized world. The reason was evident to the far-seeing. Winnipeg and Manitoba were producing nothing for export at that time and all available money for speculation was practically invested.

It was a trying time of suspense. Major Semple, however, was as buoyantly confident as ever and when the last kick of reckless speculation in Winnipeg followed the ominous calm of January and February, the townsite of Edmonton was placed on the market, and he plunged into the vortex of the situation with all the fever of his temperament and all the money that he could raise by importunity or covenant.

The story of the Edmonton boom in Winnipeg in the spring of

150

1882 has often been told. It was the spirit of boom speculation gone mad. It was the despairing effort of some to whom the stern fact had come home that as great as western Canada was, that not until settlement had come and crops were grown could the current values of property be maintained in a young country. The real estate situation in Winnipeg in the latter part of February, 1882, was at a tension. Men hoped against hope and when the townsite of Edmonton was placed on the market, to some it was a renewal of the buoyant conditions of the previous December, and to others an opportunity to redeem themselves by quick turn-overs in a boom situation. Crowds filled the streets before popular real estate offices or thronged the corridors and sitting rooms of the hotels and the most bewildering business situation in Canada's history ensued.

Only a limited number of Edmonton town lots were placed on the market and these doubled in price before noon and trebled before nightfall. All night long buying and selling took place in hotels and restaurants. Next day the excitement increased and lots that twenty-four hours before had been purchased for $100 were now being sold for $800 and $1,000. The speculative element was fast becoming glutted with Edmonton lots.

Strange to say, the first person in Winnipeg to fully grasp at the moment the utter madness of a boom was the young Canadianized English girl, Marion Semple. As young as she was, she had watched clear-eyed and clear-headed the vicissitudes of her father's business life in Canada. Firmly as she believed with the optimism of the West and of youth in the rapid growth of the country, she had painfully become convinced that as far as business investment was concerned, her father was the veriest tyro. She instinctively realized also that he was a born gambler.

Major Semple left the second day of the boom for the Parish of St. Andrews to round up some old retired Hudson's Bay Company officers. He was persuaded he could purchase on reasonable terms the buildings of these officers in a place they looked upon as a mere fur trading post.

"You have a general power of attorney, Marion," he said. "If you have an undoubted chance of a grand coup, exercise that power unhesitatingly."

She did. She sent at once for St. John Selwyn. He hadn't seen her for weeks.

"Now, no nonsense, St. John," as she drew her hand from the vice-like grip that attempted to draw her to him. "Things are too serious. This Edmonton boom is going to . . . is going to 'bust,' as you call it, and I want to get father from under before the whole thing tumbles."

"Aw! You know, bah George . . ." stammered Selwyn protestingly.

"I'm not going to try and convince you," she persisted. "You are as mad as the rest. I simply say I know it. A spectator sees the game and I've been watching father's game since I've been in short skirts. The only difference is that the whole town is now playing it. I want

In 1880, butter was a delicacy, as revealed by this advertisement in the *Winnipeg Times*.

In the nineteenth century, European Christmas cards were considered to be the most stylish and desirable. They also were expensive. This advertisement is from the *Winnipeg Times* in 1882.

This cartoon dates
from 1912 when the West was
booming.

to get him from under and I want you to help me. I want you to sell every foot of father's interests in Edmonton within two hours."

St. John Selwyn tried to argue, which showed his lack of knowledge of the mystery that came on earth with the advent of Mother Eve.

"It simply means this, St. John," said Miss Semple, as the lines about the girlish lips grew strongly defined, "Unless you sell out and unless we sell out for father, all of us will be bankrupt. A nice situation — a bankrupt wishing to marry a bankrupt's daughter. That would spell our parting and the parting, dear, might as well begin right now."

St. John Selwyn did the quickest thinking of record in the heavy-brained line of Yorkshire Selwyns. "Well, I suppose I shall have to," he ruefully muttered as he looked into the determined eyes of the woman he loved.

Major Semple made $28,545.54 and St. John Selwyn made $9,445 out of the Edmonton boom that afternoon.

When Major Semple returned late that evening, the joyous purchaser of six Jasper Avenue lots in the town of Edmonton at $200 per lot, and heard of the action of his attorney, he threw about the neatest imitation of sixteen different kinds of fits that his friends had ever seen. He said things that were unprintable, things very unbecoming an officer and a gentleman. He was milder at lunch next day and inclined to graciousness at dinner. He had been down town and discovered that the Edmonton boom had "bust" during the night. A marvellous psychological change had come over the real estate situation and before noon, "you couldn't give an Edmonton lot away if there was a shadow of a covenant even on the next block."

"We'll keep those purchases I made from the Hudson's Bay people," the major said, grimly throwing the deeds into his strong box as they were packing up in readiness for the flitting back to the homeland, for Marion and Selwyn were to be married in the following May.

Major Semple kept the lots for twenty years and last Christmas the venerable old British soldier called his matronly daughter to him in the manor house of the Selwyns where he was spending the holiday. "I just wish to call your attention, Marion, to the fact that my judgement was right about the value of Edmonton property in the spring of 1882. I have just received an offer for those Jasper Avenue lots in Edmonton, in Canada. You remember when I bought them in the spring, a few months before you were married. I have been offered $1,000 a foot for them. You see, my dear, that my business judgement was always my strong point."

Mrs. Selwyn never smiled and the old gentleman went on complacently, "I have determined to give my eldest granddaughter my Edmonton estate." His daughter's eyes softened and her heart went back to the ice-bound Red River illuminated by the flickering Northern Lights, and she whispered: "Christmas is such a blessed time, dear father."

The Wild West

Just after Christmas, 1885, C.E.D. Wood editorialized in The Macleod Gazette on the way the town had celebrated the Yuletide season.

Christmas is very properly considered a time when a little more license than usual should be given. If a certain number of people believe that they can extract more enjoyment from a state of hilarious intoxication than in any other way, let them do it, as long as they do not interfere with others who may think differently. If some people can squeeze amusement out of chewing one another's ears off, by all means let them chew, and gouge and bite and scratch. So long as they only kill one or two among themselves in this way, no one would grieve very much. No one would care to interfere with such pleasant little pastimes as those indicated above.

But we do draw the line at shooting.

Both on Christmas eve and on Christmas night, peaceful citizens were aroused from their sleep by the howling of a drunken mob. This was not all. Shot followed shot in rapid succession, and the fusilade was kept up until morning. The shots were not harmless ones either, but were ball cartridges, fired from forty-five calibre revolvers. On Xmas night, the precaution of firing into the air was not even taken, but the shots were fired right down the main street. And even if they were fired into the air, the danger from a falling ball is just as great as direct from the pistol.

We have not the least hesitation in saying that such a method of enjoyment (?) is disgraceful in the extreme, worthy only of the lowest class of the western desperado, who makes a big noise to give people the impression that he is real bad. It matters not to such men that some of those shots might kill some one on the street, or even penetrate a dwelling house, and perhaps kill a woman or a child. What care such men for women or children? They must appear bad no matter whether school keeps or not. Steps will be taken to see that the performance of last Thursday and Friday nights is not repeated, and sure and speedy punishment will be meted out to those who cannot use a privilege without seriously abusing it. *Verbum sap.*

The Christmas Carol

With no Christmas movies to attend, no festive ballets, no specials on T.V., townsfolk sometimes went to extra ordinary lengths to provide their own holiday entertainment.

One of Canada's most prolific and gifted writers, Nellie L. McClung drew upon her own experiences to tell this story. It occurred in Manitou, Manitoba about 1900.

cross the road from our house stood a little weather-beaten dwelling whose occupants came and went frequently. It seemed to harbour a strange contagion of impermanency, though it was an honest enough little house with its L-shaped walls and lean-to kitchen. At the time of which I write its tenants were a Mr. and Mrs. Vander and their three children. The father was a meek little man who had a Byronic face, who spoke beautiful English and read from the classics. The mother went out working by the day, a tired draggled woman, who accepted her lot in life without complaint. The family consisted of three handsome children; the eldest girl had a gift for music and art, which won for her an honorable place in the local school.

There was a scarcity of teachers in the Manitou District at this time, and when I discovered that Mr. Vander had once taught in a boys' school, I thought we might be able to get a temporary certificate for him and get him installed in one of the country schools. I knew he could teach well if he wanted to. His wife was more enthusiastic than he when I went over and made the suggestion. When I mentioned the usual salary of fifty dollars a month, I could see that he was not impressed.

"Madam, I have pride. I have pride of ancestry, nationality and tradition. I am proud of my heritage of English literature and if you and my wife will refrain from interrupting me I will take you into my confidence. I have a plan to help my fellow men, an infinitely better plan than this teaching scheme, one into which I can put my whole heart."

He was off on his magic carpet, leaving the cares of the world behind him, and strangely enough he was able to make us listen.

His plan was, in brief, to give readings from Dickens' "Christmas Carol" two days before Christmas. He would make his own tickets and send the children out to sell them:

Marley's Ghost.

This illustration appeared in an 1868 edition of Dicken's *A Christmas Carol.*

155

AN EVENING WITH DICKENS — THE CHRISTMAS CAROL
Interpreted by Frederick T. Vander
late of Drury Lane, London
Manitou Town Hall
Admission by Ticket Only

The cold December night came down in the best Manitoba tradition, a windy night, with stars hanging low in a sky of cold steel. A cold night never held any of us in if we wanted to go out so the McClung family was represented by three members — Jack, Florence and myself. The head of the house had a curling game at the rink and pleaded his case by saying that he must have exercise. Jack would have gladly gone with his father, but I coaxed him to come with us with the argument that the literary arts must be encouraged, and everyone should hear the Christmas Carol at least once a year.

The hall was a draughty place, heated by one stove in the middle of the room. A straggling audience occupied the zone around the stove and a fair pile of firewood promised a continuance of heat. (The newspaper said in its account of the gathering that "the intelligence of the audience made up for the smallness of its numbers.")

Promptly at eight o'clock the Interpreter, Mr. Frederick T. Vander, in evening dress, came out from the back room with a copy of the "Christmas Carol" in his hand. He was in good voice and looked like a perfect Bob Cratchet. He even had the white scarf inside his coat with its fluttering white ends. I resolutely put aside the opinion I had of him as a husband and father and settled down to enjoy the performance.

"Marley was dead," he began, and we were off. Let the wind blow, let the tin roof crackle and buckle, we were listening to an immortal tale. The little man knew how to present his story. He played all parts with equal facility; he was Scrooge, tight-fisted and wizened, harsh of voice and hard of heart; he was the timid little clerk trying to warm himself at the candle. He was the fog that came pouring into every chink, "making the houses across the street into mere phantoms." And how well he did the nephew all in a glow of good fellowship who came in to wish old Scrooge a merry Christmas! — which he defined as — "A kind forgiving charitable time ... when men and women open their shut-up hearts freely and think of the people below them as fellow passengers to the grave, and not another race bound on other journeys."

So intent were we on the story that no one noticed that the fire was burning low and it was not until the knocker on the door changed to Marley's face that someone on the outer fringe of the audience came forward and mended the fire noisily. The Interpreter glared at the interruption but resumed the story. The caretaker of the hall, Mr. Miller, roused to his duty by this alien hand laid on his stove, reasserted his authority by piling in more wood and more wood, and soon the crackling of the stove joined the rumbling of the tin roof. The audience stretched their chilly hands to the warmth and went adventuring on the high seas where grizzled men raised their voices in praise of Christmas.

It was not until the Second Spirit entered that we began to feel sudden draughts across the floor as certain members of the audience drifted out. Each time the door opened a blast from the Arctic Circle smote us. Then, by sign language, we urged Mr. Miller to greater efforts.

About ten o'clock when Scrooge and the Spirit of Christmas Present went through the streets and saw "The brightness of the roaring fires in kitchens where preparations for the Christmas dinner were going on and tantalizing smells of turkey and sage came through the doors as happy children ran out to meet their cousins arriving" — it was then I missed my first born who had noiselessly departed, but Florence stayed on. She was drawn as far into her coat as she could get and had gathered her feet under her for warmth.

We lost another detachment when the Cratchets sat down to the goose, and the young Cratchets crammed spoons into their mouths lest they should shriek for goose before their turn came to be helped.

By the time the last Spirit had taken Scrooge to see his grisly ending, the wind had risen to new heights, and not only the tin roof, but the timbers of the hall creaked and groaned, and made strange and threatening noises. The audience were all around the stove now and the Speaker was with us too. He had put on his overcoat and mittens.

We looked in vain for Mr. Miller, but it appeared that he had gone, and evidently had taken the last of the firewood with him, so there we were at the end of our resources, but not the end of the story.

We saw it out; we stayed until the end, which came about eleven; and in spite of the cold and the burned out fire, the crackling roof and the bitter wind that found out every crack in the old Orange Hall, in spite of everything, we felt the thrill of the awakened soul of Ebenezer Scrooge, as the magic of Christmas ran in our veins, setting at naught the discomfort of the hour.

Since then, many many times we have heard the story told in the golden voices of John and Lionel Barrymore, heard it in warm rooms brightened by wood fires, with plates of apples waiting for us, and the fragrance of coffee on the air. But it was on that cold night in the old Orange Hall in Manitou that Florence and I, numb to the knees, really entered into the magic circle of the Dickens' Fellowship, and we felt ever since that we have the right to gather with the faithful wherever they are.

Ad astra per aspera.

Letter from a Barr Colonist

Six months after arriving at the future site of Lloydminster, Mrs. Alice Rendell wrote this letter home to friends in England. Her house, which she named "Doris Court," was on the outskirts of the town.

Doris Court, Lloydminster,
Brittannia, Sask., N.W.T.
Canada.
[January, 1904]

ear Friends,
According to promise I am going to do my best to give you, to the best of my ability, a graphic account of how we spent our first Christmas in Lloydminster. I think as Christmas approached we all rather dreaded it knowing how this special season brings with it so forcibly the memory of all the home gatherings in the Old Country. Fortunately, we personally, are far too busy in our surrounding to brood over vain regrets and Christmas Day was upon us almost before we could realize the fact. There was service at 11:00 o'clock a.m. and at 5:00 p.m. the "Festivities" started.

Thanks to the generosity of Messers. Hall Scott and Co. who have just completed a very large building for General Stores, the Gathering of the Colonists took place there and it is certainly owing to their great kindness that our Christmas and New Year was spent so pleasantly and happily. The first item on the programme was a big feed followed by a capital concert divided into two parts. After the first half had been successfully carried through came a large Christmas tree very prettily decorated, the little gifts being distributed by an ideal "Santa Claus". I need scarcely say how delighted the little ones were. The whole proceedings were brought to a close about 11:30 p.m. after a most enjoyable social gathering and the first Christmas in Lloydminster is a thing of the past but nevertheless it will be remembered by all who were present as a bright and happy one, the more so as it was unexpected and so well carried out. The effect it had upon us was that we all felt cheered by this little excitement after all we had previously passed through and somehow "longed for more".

Thanks again to Messrs. Hall Scott and Co. another happy gathering was arranged for New Years Eve and yet another on New

Years Day. They not only gave the use of their splendid building for a dance but undertook all arrangements and issued a general invitation and welcome to all. The room was very prettily decorated and the floor well waxed. The band consisted of several violins, two coronets, and harmonium. We started dancing at 8:30 p.m. and after a most enjoyable evening broke up at about 4:30 a.m. We all felt years younger. We wound up with Sir Roger and Auld Lang Syne and walked back to Doris Court in brilliant moonlight, arriving home as the clock struck 5:00 a.m. The next evening (Saturday) there was an excellent concert at the conclusion of which there was an impromptu dance, this being the last in Messrs. Hall Scott and Co's. spacious building. You will see that our Christmas and New Year was by no means dull or miserable, nor were our dear absent ones forgotten.

When Alice Rendell spent her first Christmas with the Barr colonists in 1903, Lloydminster was just a collection of tents and clapboard buildings.

Christmas at the Royal Hotel

Each hotel in a prairie town tried to outdo the others in offering a wide variety of plain and exotic food for Christmas dinner.
This was the menu at the Royal Hotel in Calgary for Christmas, 1891.

Soup	Fish
Hare Oysters	Rock Cod, Bechmal Sauce

Entrees
Lamb Chops Petit, Pois Pen	Oyster Volsa Vent, au Neiga
Macaroni and Cheese	

Boiled
Capon et Pore Salee	Ham a la Westhalia
Chicken Salad	Celery

Game
Antelope, with Black Currant Jelly	Black Bear with Red Currant Jelly
Partridge with Bread Sauce	
Haunch of Venison with Port Wine Sauce	

Roasts
Sirloin of Beef.	Turkey with Cranberry Sauce
Yorkshire Pudding	Domestic Duck.
Goose with Apple Sauce	Grape Jelly

Cold and Ornamental Dishes
Suckling Pig. a la Jardinere	Ham, Garnis de Gelee
Tongue a l'Ecarlate	Saddle of Mutton, a la Francaise
Turkey with Truffles	

Vegetables
Mashed Potatoes   Boiled Potatoes   Tomatoes   String Beans

Pastry
Green Apple. Mince and Cream Pies	English Plum Pudding. Brandy Sauce

Jellies
Port Wine   Sherry Wine   Brandy and Lemon

Dessert
Christmas Cake   Macaroon Pyramids   Chalotte Russe
Whip Sylabub   Assorted Cakes   Oranges   Apples   Grapes
Walnuts   Almonds   Filberts   Brazils   Raisins

Black Tea   Green Tea   Coffee

Royal Hotel, Calgary.

First-class in every particular.
Close to the Depot and in the centre business portion.

1891   **INGRAM & CLARKE, Prop'rs.**

The Royal Hotel in Calgary was proud of the variety of meals it could offer at Christmas.

Jellied Cabbage Salad

This appeared in the Farm and Ranch Review *just before Christmas, 1909.*

Soften half a package (one ounce) of gelatine in half a cup of cold water and dissolve in a cup and a half of boiling water; let cool a little, then add three cups of chopped cabbage, two green peppers, chopped fine, a teaspoonsful of salt, half a cup of sugar, one-fourth of a cup of lemon juice and half a cup of vinegar. Mix together thoroughly and turn into a quart brick mould or a bread pan. When cold and firm cut into cubes about two inches in diameter. Set on lettuce leaves.

Christmas Fruit Cake

Also from the Farm and Ranch Review, *this appeared in December of 1911.*

Two cups butter, two cups brown sugar, one cup molasses, five eggs, one cup milk, four and one half cups flour, two cups chopped raisins, two cups currants, one cup dates, one cup chopped figs, one cup dried apples, one teaspoon cinnamon, one teaspoon nutmeg, half teaspoon cloves, one teaspoon salt, a pound of lemon, orange and citron combined in any proportion to suit the taste, one cup walnuts, one cup almonds, one teaspoon soda, two teaspoons cream of tartar.

Chop up dried apples and stew them in the molasses until they are clear and tender, adding water if necessary to keep from scorching. Chop fruits, peels and nuts, combine, and sprinkle generously with flour. Sift the spices, soda and cream of tartar with the flour. Cream the butter, add sugar, gradually; break the eggs in and beat thoroughly, add the milk, then the molasses and apples, which have been allowed to cool; next the flour gradually. When nearly all the flour is in add a cup full of fruits, etc., alternately with a little flour until all is used up. Line cake tins with buttered paper, fill two-thirds full and bake in a moderate oven, until done when tested with a broom corn.

Ah, the poor, lonely bachelor! This
cartoon was published in Regina
in 1912.

Lonely at Christmas

Written in 1906 by R.C. "Bob" Edwards, one of Canada's most gifted writers of satire and humor, this item reflects the author's innermost feelings. Edwards himself was the lonely man described in the article, a solitary bachelor living in a Calgary hotel room.

This is the season of the year, Christmas coming on and so forth, when we most envy the folk with nice cosy little homes of their own. You who have your own fireside do not realize what you possess. You do not know what it is to go without having anyone to say to you, "Goodbye, will you be gone long?" or to come back without anyone to welcome you and say, "Oh, how late you are!" Think at this time of the year of the many young men far from their own homes back east, living in Calgary with no place to go of an evening, moping in their $8 a month rooms reading *Frenzied Finance* or hanging around hotels hitting up the booze. Give them a thought.

It needs only a little friendly interest to make better and happy the solitary individual who lives near you, who is abandoned to himself and to the inspiration of his unutterable ennui. The solitary youths, far from their paternal hearths, have a rocky old time struggling with the discouragements of their existence here, exposed to the temptations of the booze shops. There are evenings upon evenings that they make bad use of for want of a better. Perhaps they are nothing to you and you are under no obligation to them, but — put yourself in their place.

Bob Edwards' Plum Pudding

This appeared in the Calgary Eye Opener, *in December of 1909.*

Take one quart of brandy, two handfuls of plums and raisins, a chunk of suet, some salt and a lot of flour. Knead the last three ingredients well together, pouring into yourself sufficient brandy to keep from getting tired.

When of sufficient consistency hang it on clothes line and beat smartly with a yule log. Roll into a round ball, try and raise it slowly above your head with one hand to see if it is heavy enough and then saturate plentifully with brandy. Set fire to the mess and serve quickly. Return to kitchen and put balance of brandy out of pain.

A Bachelor's Dream

This bit of whimsey is based upon an often repeated story of pioneer life, but whether it is fact or fiction the reader will have to judge. It appeared in the Alberta Folklore Quarterly in 1945.

One Christmas Eve, a CPR bachelor sat in his lonely quarters in a small prairie town. He was in a retrospective mood, and there passed through his mind visions of Christmases of the long ago when there was always a joyous throng gathered around the gift-laden tree. He recalled letters addressed in cramped little hands to Santa Claus, thought lovingly of dear faces of those far-off days, and felt very dreary. Thinking, too, of his friends who had recently forsaken the ranks of bachelordom, he was overpowered by a sensation of unutterable loneliness.

Throwing on his greatcoat and cap he went out into what seemed to him a cold and cheerless night. Wandering down the street, and entering a clothing store, he bought a pair of lady's silk stockings, took them back to his room, hung them in front of the fireplace and pinned to them the following note:

"Dear Santa Claus — Please try and fill these for me before next Christmas."

Christmas Dinner

In about 1913, Peter McArthur was invited to Christmas dinner by Judge Charles Stuart of Calgary. In gratitude, he penned this poem.

Dear Charles —

The torpor of the feast
Still steeps me in its charm,
As here I sit beside the stove
Contented, placid, warm,
And wonder if my gastric power
Is competent to wage
Digestive war 'gainst this assault
Of turkey stuffed with sage.

And if it isn't — "What the hell."
Just let the nightmares prance
This night upon my stomach's full
And round protuberance;
For I have had a jolly time,
And "Peace on earth" I sing,
"Good will to men," with hope that they
Have also had their fling.

'Twas one o'clock when I went down
With vaulting appetite,
And sat with Dickey at my left,
The artist at my right;
Hardcastle worked the carving knife,
Miss Peck a welcome smiled,
While Gertrude piled side dishes full,
And giggled as she piled.

With clatter loud the fray began,
We wrought with might and main
And knives and forks and everything
A victory to gain.
Cranberry sauce was like the dew
When fierce the sun doth shine;
And celery went down like corn
Before devouring kine.

But soon the ardor that inspired
The first assault was spent,
And on us all began to fall
The spirit of Content.
We laid our knives and forks aside,
Each heaved a happy sigh,
Then took a swig of cider (hard)
And wrestled with the pie.

Next came the oranges and nuts,
With Dickey's flow of jests,
And squirmings around in corsets and
The opening of vests;
And then reluctantly we rose
And up the groaning stairs,
With lagging feet we slowly climbed,
And sought our various lairs.

Yes, I was full! I am so still!
Nor deem that fulness sin,
Though Faith and Fasts go hand in hand,
To feasts my Hope I pin,
In all the world I doubt if there's
A saint with soul benign
Whose feeling of good will to men
Is more sincere than mine.

And so, dear boy, I write to you
To wish you well and say
I hope that you abdominal
Distension feel today,
To hell with liver, blues and dumps!
Who cares for griping bile?
Tonight I'll pledge you as of old
In foaming Staten Isle.

What matters it if now and then
The wolf should near us snarl?
We're better than the candid fool
Who bugs his golden "bar'l";

Christmas in the West

And while to you I drain a health
Of "Johnny's" wholesome beer,
I'll wish you happiness enough
To fill the coming year.

As for myself I've but to say,
Let *empires* rise or fall,

For any bluff that Fate may give
I'll have the nerve to call,
I'll play the limit come what will
And back the hands I draw
If Heaven will grant me appetite
When'er I go to draw.

Yours cheerfullee
McArthur, P.

CHRISTMAS DINNER AT SNIDER & CURLETTES 1901.

When Calgary photographers
Snider and Curlette had a
Christmas dinner in 1901, they
recorded the event for posterity.
Note that E. B. Curlette, front
left, holds a cord to operate the
camera. The meal was held at
their studio in the Wallace Block
on Stephen Avenue.

" 'Tis the Season . . ."

As a finale to this book, its author and editor, Hugh A. Dempsey, recalls his Christmases as a child during the Great Depression. Born on a farm near Edgerton, Alberta, he moved to Edmonton at the age of five and experienced Christmases as part of a family on relief. Not until 1939 was his father able to land a permanent job, first with the Alberta government and later as a federal Customs' officer.

n the early 1930s we were hailed out, dried out, and frozen out on our farm south of Edgerton, Alberta, on McCafferty Flats. I was born in the year of the Wall Street crash so I didn't know much about what was going on, but I did learn later that 1934 had been the last straw for the Dempsey family. Not only had we been dried out again, but dad lost his job as secretary-treasurer of the municipality when the small office, which was on our property, burned to the ground.

That's when dad decided to move to the Peace River country. At that time stories were being told of the bumper crops up there during a period when the drouth-stricken prairies were blowing away. So dad sold off most of our possessions in the fall for almost nothing and hired a trucker to take the rest of our stuff to Edmonton. His idea was that the family would stay there while he went north with Murdo Fraser, our hired man, to find a farm for us. For the move we managed to bring along the family pet, named The Old Cat, and three mink that dad wanted to use as breeding stock in the north.

We must have looked like a bunch of hillbillies when we arrived at our small rented house on 91st Street. In fact, some of the neighbours' kids were not allowed to play with us. I usually went barefoot in summer and patched up hand-me-downs were a normal part of my attire. In winter I wore moccasins with rubbers pulled over them and sealer rings to keep them from falling off. I don't recall what anyone else wore but we were all a pretty scruffy bunch. Within a week one of the mink got away and ran into a barn next door. We almost had to tear the place apart before we caught the animal, and then we decided to get rid of all three.

In the meantime, dad had left for the north but he ran into an early fall snowstorm and had to turn back. He then gave up on the

These toys were collected by the Calgary Junior Red Cross in 1923 for distribution to needy children.

Peace River country and decided to stay in Edmonton. So there we were — mom, dad and four boys — in the middle of the Depression, no job, and only the limited proceeds from the farm sale to keep us going during the winter.

That's when I remember my first Christmas. We had no turkey that year — for the first time since mom and dad were married. In fact, there wasn't enough money for essentials much less the luxuries that one associates with the festive season. Yet as a kid that loss didn't seem to be too important to me. After all, we were together as a family, we had a warm house, and we weren't starving. Rather, the thing that stood out in my mind was a Christmas present I received from the lady next door, a kindly person I remember only as Mrs. Fields. She gave me a velvet Popeye doll, with his squinty eye, sailor's cap, and even with a pipe sticking out of his mouth. It was a wonderful gift for a five-year-old and I fell in love with it. I talked to it, took it to bed with me, and would not even let people take the pipe out of its mouth. It was my best pal almost until I went to school.

We had to go on relief later that winter when the money ran out. Dad was a very proud person who hated welfare, but there was no other way, for jobs just weren't available. Only in later years did I realize how tough things really had been. We got $40 a month relief money, with $15 of that going for rent — later increasing to $20 when we moved to a bigger house. As relief recipients we got our clothes and shoes free, but they were all the same and as soon as a person put them on, everyone knew they were on relief.

To make matters worse, in the spring of 1935 dad got a job at Hayward Lumber Co., but on his first day a pile of lumber fell on him and broke his ankle. He was in hospital for a while and then on crutches for the better part of a year. That meant we were taken off relief and put on workmen's compensation. They also paid us $40 a month but there were no food coupons and the money had to cover the cost of clothes as well. It meant that instead of a Sunday roast, mom bought ends and scraps of meat for a stew. It also meant strict rationing and no new clothes for an entire year. Obviously, Christmas in 1935 was celebrated under even more straitened conditions for us than it had been the previous year.

After that, things got a little better. When we went back on relief, it was almost a bonanza to get a clothing allowance and food coupons. Besides, I was in school by this time and once a day all of us kids on relief were given a glass of milk to drink at recess time. In the meantime, we were always busy trying to raise money. We went down to the city dump to find rags that could be washed and sold to garages and on Sunday mornings we went to a favourite parking and drinking place overlooking the North Saskatchewan River and looked for beer bottles. These could be sold for 20 cents a dozen. That summer, when I was six, I also got a job as helper on a milk wagon. Rising at 5 a.m., I met the milkman after he had hitched up his horses and brought the wagon to his house for breakfast. From there we went on his route, he doing one side of the street and me the other. When we finished at noon, I got paid a nickel and sometimes a ten-cent quart of milk besides.

When dad got off crutches, he began doing carpentry work, selling ironing boards door to door, and digging gardens, so we all profitted by the extra income to supplement the relief money.

Regardless of these adversities, my recollections of Christmases in the Depression years weren't of hard times or being deprived. And this was not just childish innocence on my part. Years later when I spoke to my mother about it, she agreed with me. "We lived a hand to mouth existence," she said, "and were run down at the heels, but we didn't think anything of it at the time. Just about everyone else we knew seemed to be in the same situation."

My memory of Christmas was going to bed so excited that I couldn't sleep. My brother Glen and I were told that Santa Claus would pass us by if we stayed awake, but the idea of sleeping at such a time seemed impossible. Mom and dad had been skillful in buying and hiding our few presents so to our knowledge everything depended upon Santa's visit. Finally, by some miracle, Christmas morning arrived and at about five o'clock my brother and I crept downstairs and into the living room. Santa had come! There, under the tree were what seemed to me to be piles and piles of presents. We nudged each other excitedly, shook a few presents, and tried to read the names on the tags. Finally, we found our Christmas stockings and darted back to our bedroom to eat the nuts and oranges while we impatiently waited for the rest of the household to awake.

It seems now that the presents themselves were less important

Biggar. 1939

Rutted with snow, the main street of Biggar, Saskatchewan was nonetheless ablaze with light for Christmas 1939.

than actually getting them. The presents, the stocking, the tree — all of these were symbols of love and family. If I try to think back about the toys I had before I was ten years old, I'm more likely to recall the little trucks I made from wood ends or the lead soldiers I stole from Kresge's department store on a dare.

With or without turkey, Christmas was a big day for us. Quite a few other farmers had been dried out in the Edgerton district and, like us, they had come to Edmonton. People like Ernie Trotter, Knutt Tangen and Jack Cram were on relief too, and sometimes came round at Christmas, as did Murdo Fraser, a bachelor who lived at the Salvation Army. As well, dad's brother Stuart and his family usually joined us. They had stayed on the farm and Christmas was a perfect time to get together.

When she could afford it, mom made a rich fruit cake in the fall and kept it in the cellar where it could age until Christmas. Then, as the holiday approached, she made the traditional plum pudding and always managed to get some small silver nickels which were scattered throughout its glutinous mass. However, the holiday really took some planning on mom's part. She had to depend upon the little money she had been able to save in the fall. It wasn't much, but enough to make our Christmas seem like something special.

Our guests usually arrived in the afternoon and us kids went out to play with our cousins or to show them our presents. Meanwhile, the women drifted off to the kitchen and the men sat around the front room smoking and talking about the farm, politics, and the hard times. There was a lot of laughter and story telling.

170

Us kids did not have skates or toboggans, but we did have some rough sleds that dad had made and if the weather was mild we could take them to the hills of the Saskatchewan River where we had a lot of fun. Otherwise, we played around the house, sharing the excitement of the holiday, smelling the aroma of food cooking in the kitchen, and looking over our presents again and again.

One special gift always arrived every year just before Christmas and was opened immediately. It was from my Grandma Sharp in Folkestone, England, and contained a bundle of British children's magazines all rolled up tight and wrapped with brown paper. I had seen a few American comic books, but these were entirely different. Tabloid in size, they were an exciting mixture of comics, stories and puzzles. Hours were spent pouring over the adventure tales and the continuing sagas of Harold Lloyd or George Formby in comic book form. And, just as important, they were exclusive to me; no other kid on the block had ever seen them. I never met my grandma, but I loved her for thinking of me at Christmas.

If we had new guests at Christmas, we would haul down the copies of Harmsworth's Encyclopedia for a guessing game. At the beginning of each new letter of the alphabet there was a third of a page filled with objects beginning with that letter. If it was "B" one was sure to find a bee, buffalo or bottle, but might have more trouble identifying a bassoon or a blunderbuss. Even with our familiarity with the encyclopedia, I don't think any of us ever identified every single item.

Finally, mom and her visitors set the dining room table, digging out her best dishes and silver. We could not afford soft drinks for Christmas, so in the fall we kids went down to the city dump looking for wine bottles which still had the corks in them. Then mom made a mild ginger beer out of wheat that friends brought from the farm and the bottles sat upside down fermenting until Christmas day. One of these was placed beside every plate.

What great fun we had opening the bottles! They were wired down to keep them from exploding and as one took the wire off, he never knew when the cork would suddenly go bang! and spray the beer all over the room. An empty glass was kept handy so the bottle could be upended into it as soon as the liquid began to bubble out.

Soon, what seemed to my youthful eyes to be piles and piles of steaming food was brought in from the kitchen. This was the occasion when the potatoes were put through the ricer to produce a fluffy white mound that seemed to collapse under the weight of the gravy. Also, a mixture of peas and carrots was always present — something we called "Presbyterian mix" for some reason or other. And if we were lucky enough to have turkey that year — like the time mom won one in a bingo game — there was sage dressing and giblet gravy, all done with that professional touch which my mother had learned while working in the kitchens of rich people in England.

The dessert at the best of times was plum pudding, fruit cake and perhaps hot mince pie. In lean years, it was plum pudding alone and somehow mom always managed the servings so that there was at least one nickel on each plate before the sauce was poured over it.

The measure of the meal was the degree of immobility it produced afterwards. Usually I stretched out on the floor to groan happily in my overstuffed and completely satiated condition. Others were equally relaxed, except for the women who seemed anxious to clear up the shambles on the table and to plunge the dishes into hot soapy water. Outside it might be cold or blizzardy, but in our little rented house, all was happy and serene. Unless they were staying overnight, our guests left soon after the dishes were done, and we all settled down in the happiness and security of family life.

That's what I call Christmas.

Below: 1803 greeting card for Christmas and New Year.

Wishing You a Merry Christmas and a Happy New Year

Notes on Sources

Some of the Christmas stories in this book have appeared in a number of sources over a period of years. Listed here, in the order of appearance, are the specific sources consulted. Every reasonable effort has been made to contact the author or publisher but in many instances a periodical has ceased publication, an author cannot be traced, or the article is out of copyright and in the public domain. However, thanks are extended to all authors and publishers who have permitted their material to be reprinted here.

"Christmas at York Factory, 1843," by Robert M. Ballantyne, *Hudson's Bay; or Everyday Life in the Wilds of North America,* London: Thomas Nelson & Sons, 1882; "Christmas at Fort Edmonton," by Paul Kane, *Wanderings of an Artist Among the Indians of North America,* London: Longmans, 1859; "At Cumberland House," by John Hunter, Papers of the Church Missionary Society, Microfilm Reel A-91, Glenbow Archives, Calgary; "Holidays at Edmonton," by Peter Erasmus, *Buffalo Days and Nights,* Calgary: Glenbow Museum, 1976; "Christmas in the Dog Days," by John McDougall, McDougall Papers, A/M 173A, Glenbow Archives, Calgary; "Christmas, 1872," by Donald Graham, *Alberta Historical Review* 11:4, Autumn 1958; "Christmas on the Plains," by James McKernan, *Farm and Ranch Review,* Calgary, Dec. 6, 1920; "Christmas at Red River Settlement," by Joseph James Hargraves, *The Winnipeg Daily Sun,* Dec. 23, 1882; "Archbishop Taché Remembers," *The Winnipeg Daily Sun,* Dec. 23, 1882; "A Christmas Letter," *The Nor'Wester,* Red River Settlement, Dec. 11, 1864; "How Riel's Prisoners Spent Christmas," by An Old Resident, *The Winnipeg Daily Sun,* Dec. 23, 1882; "A Dinner to Remember," *The Winnipeg Daily Times,* Dec. 24, 1884; "Christmas, 1871," by Frank Larned Hunt, *The Manitoban,* Winnipeg, Dec. 23, 1871; "My Darling Liz," by Richard Barrington Nevitt, Nevitt Papers, Glenbow Archives, Calgary; "Tragedy at Fort Macleod," by Cecil Denny, *The Law Marches West,* Toronto: J. M. Dent & Sons, 1939; "Christmas at Swan River," by William Parker, Letter, Parker to his mother, Jan. 4, 1876, Parker Papers, Glenbow Archives, Calgary; "Christmas at Fort Calgary," *The Toronto Mail,* Feb. 19, 1877; "Christmas Greetings," *The Macleod Gazette,* Dec. 23, 1882; "Cricket at Christmas," *The Macleod Gazette,* Dec. 29, 1885; "Mess Menu," *The Macleod Gazette,* Dec. 31, 1891; "Celebrating the 'Big Holy Day'," by John W. Tims, *Lethbridge Herald,* Dec. 12, 1931; "A Christmas Letter," *Calgary Herald,* Jan. 16, 1894; "Christmas Day," by Mike Mountain Horse, *My People the Bloods,* Calgary: Glenbow Museum, 1979; "My Dear Child," by John W. Tims, Tims Papers, A/T586, Glenbow Archives, Calgary.

"Christmas, 1880," *Winnipeg Daily Times,* Dec. 25, 1880; "A Homestead Christmas," by Nellie L. McClung, *Clearing in the West,* Toronto: Thomas Allen, 1935; "Dear Grandma," by Maryanne Caswell, *Pioneer Girl,* Toronto: McGraw-Hill Co., 1964; "The Cowboy's Christmas," *Calgary Tribune,* Jan. 3, 1894; "Letter to the Lonely," by Belle MacDonald, *Farm and Ranch Review,* Calgary, December 1906; "Christmas Day for Lonely People," by Kathleen Redman Strange, *Lethbridge Herald,* Dec. 21, 1929; "The Bachelor Homesteader," by John Wilson, *The Grain Growers' Guide,* Winnipeg, Sept. 20, 1911; "A Parson's Diary," by C. Travers Melly, *Occasional Paper No. 17,* Archbishops' Western Canada Fund, Camberwell, Eng.: H. B. Skinner & Co., March 1915; "Letters From the West," by Monica Hopkins, Hopkins Papers, Glenbow Archives, Calgary; "How to Prepare a Turkey," by Helen Wainwright, *Farm and Ranch Review,*

Calgary, Dec. 5, 1911; "North-West of Sixteen," by James G. MacGregor, *North-West of Sixteen,* Toronto: McClelland & Stewart, 1958; "Christmas Stuffing," by Leta R. Porter, *Farm and Ranch Review,* Dec. 1, 1930; "My Best Christmas," by Doris Wright, *The Grain Growers' Guide,* Winnipeg, Dec. 7, 1910; "A Hard Times Christmas," by Amy J. Ross, *The Grain Growers' Guide,* Winnipeg, Dec. 14, 1921; "Useful Christmas Gifts," *Farm and Ranch Review,* Nov. 25, 1925; "The Christmas Tree," *Scandia Since Seventeen,* Scandia: Scandia Historical Committee, 1978; "Norwegian Pioneers," by Ragna Steen and Magda Hendrickson, *Pioneer Days in Bardo, Alberta,* Tofield: Historical Society of Beaver Hills Lake, 1946; "Men in Sheepskin Coats," by Vera Lysenko, *Men in Sheepskin Coats,* Toronto: Ryerson Press, 1947; "An Icelandic Christmas," by Walter J. Lindal, *The Saskatchewan Icelanders; a Strand of the Canadian Fabric,* Winnipeg: Columbia Press, 1955; "Holidays for an English Settler," by Kathleen Redman Strange, *With the West in her Eyes,* Toronto: George J. McLeod Ltd., 1937, reprinted by permission of Macmillan of Canada, a division of Gage Publishing Ltd.; "Behind the Sateen Curtain," by Margaret Parker, *The Country Guide and Nor-'West Farmer,* Winnipeg, December 1936; "How to Make a Santa Claus Constume," by Mrs. E. F. Ashby, *Farm and Ranch Review,* Calgary, Nov. 26, 1928; "Christmas Consolation," by Leta R. Porter, *Farm and Ranch Review,* Dec. 1, 1930; "A Christmas Romance in Real Estate," by Charles Lewis Shaw, *The Winnipeg Telegram,* Dec. 24, 1910; "The Wild West," *The Macleod Gazette,* Dec. 29, 1885; "The Christmas Carol," by Nellie L. McClung, *The Stream Runs Fast; My Own Story,* Toronto: Thomas Allen Ltd., 1945; "Letter from a Barr Colonist," by Alice Rendell, *Alberta Historical Review* 11:1, Winter 1963; "Christmas at the Royal Hotel," *Calgary Tribune,* Dec. 30, 1891; "Lonely at Christmas," by R. C. "Bob" Edwards, *Calgary Eye Opener,* Dec. 2, 1906; "Bob Edwards' Plum Pudding," *Calgary Eye Opener,* Dec. 18, 1909; "Christmas Dinner," by Peter McArthur, McArthur Papers, D821.91/M116, Glenbow Archives, Calgary; "A Bachelor's Dream," *Alberta Folklore Quarterly,* Edmonton, December 1945; " 'Tis the Season . . .," by Hugh A. Dempsey, previously unpublished.

Notes on Sources: Illustrations

Many of the decorations which appear in the margins, i.e. Santa Claus, bells, trees, etc., are from a rare volume, *Stock Illustrations for the Printer and Advertiser,* published in the 1920s by Stovel Co. Ltd. of Winnipeg.

Abbreviations used are as follows: GAI — Glenbow-Alberta Institute, Calgary; PAC — Public Archives of Canada, Ottawa; PAM — Provincial Archives of Manitoba, Winnipeg; and SAB — Saskatchewan Archives Board, Regina.

1. GAI, *Harper's Weekly,* June 16, 1877; 2. GAI. NA-1754-4; 3. GAI, An. 59.39.20; 7. GAI, *Hudson's Bay, or Everyday Life in the Wilds of North America,* by R. M. Ballantyne (London 1848); 9. GAI, NA-1408-3; 11. GAI, NA-1406-152, *London Graphic,* Christmas Issue 1881; 12 & 13. GAI, *The Rainbow in the North,* by S. Tucker (London 1851); 15. GAI, NA-1406-153, *Ballou's Pictorial Drawing-Room Companion,* 1854; 18. GAI, NA-1406-23, *Harper's Monthly,* October 1860; 21. GAI, NA-1406-154, *London Graphic,* Aug. 19, 1876; 22. GAI, NA-1406-160, *Harper's Weekly,* Jan. 6, 1883; 23. GAI, NA-1406-157, *London Graphic,* Aug. 16, 1884; 26. GAI, NA-1406-82, *Harper's Weekly,* Oct. 13, 1877; 28. GAI, WR.61.32.48; 30. GAI, NA-1406-6; 34. GAI, WR.61.32.46; 38. GAI, *The Nor-Wester,* Dec. 11, 1864; 39. GAI, NA-1406-80, *London Graphic,* Feb. 26, 1881; 40. GAI, NA-1406-155. 41. PAM, Bannatyne family 103; 42. GAI, A.60.51.22; 43 top. GAI, *The Nor-Wester,* Dec. 11, 1864; 43 bottom. GAI, *The Nor-Wester,* Dec. 24, 1861; 45. GAI, NA-1406-162; 46. GAI, NA-1406-161; 48. GAI, Art No. 472; 49. GAI, NA-1406-158; 52, 54 & 57. GAI, Nevitt collection; 59. GAI, NA-2235-15; 63. GAI, NA-9-16; 66. GAI, NA-1754-5 & 7; 68. GAI, NA-444-1; 71. GAI, NA-695-55; 73. GAI, NA-1020-18; 74. GAI, WeJ.61.101.2; 77. GAI, NA-1406-156, *Harper's Weekly,* Jan. 17, 1885; 78. GAI, NA-2449-14; 79. GAI, *Grain Growers' Guide,* Dec. 1, 1926; 80. GAI, Hil.63.6; 83. GAI, NC-22-78; 84. GAI, *Regina Leader,* Dec. 18, 1912; 87. GAI, *Grain Growers' Guide,* Dec. 15, 1909; 89. GAI, NA-3251-14; 90. GAI, NA-2520-19; 92. GAI, NA-2497-2; 95. GAI, *Grain Growers' Guide,* Dec. 6, 1916; 97. GAI, *Grain Growers' Guide,* Dec. 6, 1911. 99. GAI, NA-1754-8; 100. PAM, Lindsay, Robert, 43; 101. GAI, *Calgary Tribune,* Dec. 19, 1888; GAI, *Calgary News-Telegram,* Dec. 23, 1913; 105. GAI, NA-2084-37; 107. PAM, Baldur-Farms, 2; 111. GAI, NA-1754-2; 112. GAI, NA-2878-39; 114. GAI, NA-2685-60; 115. GAI, *Grain Growers' Guide,* Dec. 6, 1911; 116. GAI, *Grain Growers' Guide,* Dec. 6, 1911; 118. GAI, *Grain Growers' Guide,* Dec. 6, 1911; 119. GAI, *Farm & Ranch Review,* Dec. 5, 1919; 120. GAI, NA-4381-2; 122. SAB, RA-4808; 124. GAI, *Winnipeg Times,* Dec. 17, 1883; 126. GAI, NA-4383-2; 127. GAI, *The Saskatchewan Icelanders, a Strand of the Canadian Fabric,* by W. J. Lindal (Winnipeg, 1955); 128. SAB, RA-8258; 129. GAI, *Medicine Hat News,* Dec. 21, 1905; 133. GAI, *Grain Growers' Guide,* Dec. 6, 1911; 135. GAI, *Grain Growers' Guide,* Dec. 15, 1909; 137. GAI, *Grain Growers' Guide,* Nov. 29, 1916; 140. H. A. Dempsey papers; 141. GAI, NA-1754-11; 142. PAM, Rapid City, Schools, 6; 144. GAI, NA-1709-57; 146. GAI, NA-3535-50; 148. GAI, NC-22-69; 150. PAC, *Winnipeg Quiz,* Oct. 26, 1878; 151 top. GAI, *Winnipeg Times,* Dec. 18, 1880; 151 bottom. GAI, *Winnipeg Times,* Dec. 22, 1882; 155. Univ. of Calgary Library, *Christmas Books,* by Charles Dickens (London 1868); 159. GAI, NA-303-72; 160. GAI, NA-430-25; 162. GAI, *Regina Leader,* Dec. 25, 1912; 166. GAI, NA-1126-11; 168. GAI, NA-2903-7; 170. GAI, NA-2870-7; 172. GAI, NA-1351-21; 173. PAC, PA-112026.

Index